"An awesome, thorough exp one of the greatest promises pastor with a true shepherd's

HENRY T. BLACKABY, PRESIDENT,
HENRY BLACKABY MINISTRIES

"Whether he is 145 feet deep in the Caribbean ocean, standing behind a pulpit, sharing Christ with someone on the street, or pursing the delightful tasks of being father and husband, John Avant's life is characterized by passion and adventure. In *The Passion Promise*, Dr. Avant takes one priceless passage of Scripture and pours a lifetime of personal experience into its mold. What emerges is precisely what Jesus intended for His followers. This is the book that needs to be read by every believer who has a serious commitment to follow Christ."

PAIGE PATTERSON, PRESIDENT,
SOUTHWESTERN BAPTIST THEOLOGICAL SEMINARY

"John Avant is my pastor, my friend, and, yes, my fellow sports junkie. This book is a reflection of his God-given gift of storytelling, offering us a road map for living a real life of passion and joy through Christ. I can't wait to share it with the college and professional athletes I know who experience the highs and lows of competition as well as the highs and lows of life."

CHRIS MORTENSEN, ESPN ANALYST

"If the Christian life has become mundane for you, this book will open a window to God's pathway to *extraordinary* living. God's promise is to lift you up and amaze you with His powerful hand. Step into the journey of seeing the improbable become the normal!"

ROBERT RECCORD, PRESIDENT,
NORTH AMERICAN MISSION BOARD

"It's amazing but not surprising how the Lord used Dr. John Avant to speak a fresh and new word to stir the hearts of believers. *The Passion Promise* challenges all who dare to go beyond the norm of being a follower of Christ. I thank God for the ministry gift of Dr. John Avant."

LEE HANEY, EIGHT-TIME WORLD BODYBUILDING CHAMPION; HOST OF *TBN'S TotaLee Fit*

"Life is too short (and too important) not to live it without 'get up and get after it' passion. John Avant's book is like kerosene to fire—read it and watch your passion for the truly important things in life explode!"

JAMES MERRITT, SENIOR PASTOR, CROSS POINTE, DULUTH, GEORGIA

"Some books convict. Others make us think. Some are more like tranquilizers. But every once in a while, a rare book comes along that makes you want to jump out of your chair and attack hell with a water pistol. *The Passion Promise* is that type of book. John Avant has a unique way of illustrating the principles of God's Word with stories that jump off the page, grab the front of your shirt, and shake you out of your comfort zone. After finishing this book, you'll find yourself wondering why you've settled for less than the high-risk, high-reward life of passion God promised. I challenge anyone to read this book and keep living the same way."

RANDY SINGER, NORTH AMERICAN MISSION BOARD

"If you're ready to rediscover your passion for life, this book sheds some great insights. It's written by an individual who walks the talk."

DAN CATHY, PRESIDENT AND COO, CHICK-FIL-A, INC.

the PASSION PROMISE

JOHN AVANT

Multnomah® Publishers *Sisters, Oregon*

THE PASSION PROMISE
published by Multnomah Publishers, Inc.

© 2004 by John Avant
International Standard Book Number: 1-59052-311-3

Cover image by Premium Stock/Corbis

Multnomah is a trademark of Multnomah Publishers, Inc., and is registered in
the U.S. Patent and Trademark Office. The colophon is a trademark of
Multnomah Publishers, Inc.

Printed in the United States of America

For information:
MULTNOMAH PUBLISHERS, INC.
POST OFFICE BOX 1720
SISTERS, OREGON 97759

Library of Congress Cataloging-in-Publication Data

Avant, John, 1960-
   The passion promise / by John Avant.
      p. cm.
   ISBN 1-59052-311-3 (pbk.)
   1. Christian life—Baptist authors.   I. Title.
   BV4501.3.A93 2004
   248.4—dc22
                     2003022863

04 05 06 07 08 09 10—10 9 8 7 6 5 4 3 2 1 0

Dedicated to my wonderful wife, Donna,
who has been my passion partner for twenty-three years,
and to our children, Christi, Amy, and Trey,
who have brought so much joy to the adventure of life.

Contents

Acknowledgments

Thanks, Mom and Dad—the Passion Promise is part of your legacy.

To the Eberts—I hardly know you, but you believed in this message enough to send the manuscript to your friend at Multnomah. Thanks for the miracle!

To the Luecks—thanks for the time you gave me in your beautiful island home, where so much of this book was written.

Meg, you're more than my assistant; you're part of our family. I could not have done this without you.

To Rosemary Preston and Dave Buck—you are great friends. You did a great job reading and proofing.

And the same to my editors, Jim Lund and Jennifer Gott, and all the wonderful people at Multnomah.

Finally, to the members of New Hope Baptist Church, who have allowed me the awesome privilege of being their pastor for these seven years. I love you and thank you for being willing to live out God's dream together.

INTRODUCTION

RISING FROM THE MAT where I had been lying, I slipped out from under the mosquito netting and stood in the darkness. I found my flashlight and walked quietly across the bamboo floor, trying not to wake the others. As if any of us would sleep much tonight! Not here. Not with what tomorrow would bring.

I walked down the wooden steps and started down the path. I looked back and could see the outline of the hut against the dark sky. It was the home of the village chief, built on stilts with a roof of straw. It had become our hotel for the evening.

A few hours before, the villagers of this Southeast Asian valley had welcomed us with ceremony and dance. Now I walked alone, keeping an eye out for snakes, until I reached the edge of a muddy stream. Looking up, I saw the incredible majesty of stars undimmed by the lights of suburbia. As my eyes adjusted to the darkness, I could just make out the outline of jungle-covered mountains all around me. I had already seen their deep green beauty on the journey a day earlier. As I stood in the moonlight, I knew that the sunrise would again reveal breathtaking scenery.

It would also reveal a village in which not one person had ever heard the name of Jesus. Not one! And with the sunrise our adventure would begin. We would seek to speak the Name to someone here for the first time. Ever.

I had no assurance how it would turn out. After all, our one interpreter was a nineteen-year-old woman, engaged to be married, who faced three years in prison if caught. When she had gone to bed, she wasn't even sure if she would continue with us.

Whether the day ahead would bring good or bad, safety or danger, I didn't know. But one thing I did know: We would be alive. *Really* alive! Making a difference. Fulfilling a mission. No going through the motions here. No, today would be a day of passion!

How did I know? Because God said so. The astounding words of a man named Paul, recorded in a letter two thousand years ago, had come off the pages of the Bible and embraced my life with their truth. Truth that spoke to the very core of my being about His love, His life, and His passion for each of His children—including me!

The apostle Paul revealed this heaven-powered passion in a prayer for the citizens of ancient Ephesus. He desperately wanted them to experience the fullness of love and blessing that God intended for them. His words then are just as powerful and stirring today:

> Now to him who is able to do immeasurably more than all we ask or imagine, according to his power that is at work within us, to him be glory in the church and in Christ Jesus throughout all generations, for ever and ever! Amen. (Ephesians 3:20–21)

In that brief passage, Paul charged the Ephesians—and through the recorded words of Scripture charges *all* believers—to bring glory to God *right now* by embracing His plan for us to experience *more than we could ever dream of* on our own.

Deep in your heart, you know you were made for more than the daily grind. Like Paul, you were created for a passionate life designed by God. Even now the Lord is calling you to that life! Calling you to trade rusty religion for radical risk. Guaranteed safety for lifelong significance. Worthless ambition for wild adventure.

Calling you to join Him right where you are.

Paul's Spirit-inspired message to the Ephesians lays the foundation for what I call the Passion Promise. It is a promise derived from Scripture and based on God's passionate heart for His children. The idea is simple, yet once fully understood and applied, it will revolutionize *everything* you think about and do for the rest of your days.

That night in the jungle, I repeated the prayer Paul sent to heaven so long ago. The words heard first by Ephesian believers were this time heard only by God. And He *did* hear. I praised Him that I could have a part in His plan. I sang. I rejoiced that I was alive, living the life my Creator had designed for me.

At first light, I joined a pilot, a power-lifter, a few businessmen, and a teenage girl and began walking down the path to find the first person in that village who would discover the passion we knew in Jesus. And then...

Wait a minute. I wouldn't want you to think that the path to a life only God can imagine is found only in some faraway place you've never heard of. Before I finish my story, we should talk about *your* story.

Do you see the trail? It's not just on the other side of the world. It stretches out before you right now! Come with me along that path and I'll make you another promise. It might be hard to believe, maybe even controversial, but it's the heart of this book: If you embrace the principles of the Passion Promise, *you will never have another boring day.*

I've been living out the Passion Promise for many years now and have found this to be true in my life and in the lives of countless others. I have seen many good days and some bad days, but I can't remember the last boring day!

Is this something you're interested in? You bet it is! Everyone wants a life that's not boring. And God, the Creator of the universe, wants it for you. He will do all He can to keep you from wandering in the wilderness for the rest of your life. His Passion Promise land is where you belong. It's home.

So how do you find home? How do you live this passionate life? Join me in the pages ahead and we'll find out.

Let the adventure begin.

chapter one

HIDDEN TREASURE

EART POUNDING, mind racing, I drove ninety miles per hour up I-85 in Atlanta.

Minutes ago my flight from Dallas had landed at Hartsfield Airport. As I stepped into the terminal, I heard the announcement: "Delta passenger John Avant, go to the nearest Delta agent for an urgent message."

I knew this couldn't be good. When they connected me and I heard my wife's voice on the phone, my fears were confirmed. It was about my good friend Dan Cathy, president of Chick-fil-A restaurants. Dan was supposed to have gone with me to Dallas for a meeting, but couldn't come. Now I wished he had.

"Dan's badly hurt," my wife said. "They don't know if he'll make it." He was being life-flighted to Grady Hospital after being seriously burned in a brush-burning accident. I must have passed a hundred cars on the freeway on my way to the hospital. An hour after landing in Atlanta, I walked into the hospital room of my strong, athletic friend—we'd recently run a half-marathon together—and saw a man fortunate to be alive. He was burned on his face, head, and both arms. He faced weeks of painful treatment and months of recovery. But he would live, and for that we all rejoiced.

Many days later, just before Dan was released from the hospital, he took me on a tour of the "torture chamber"—the room where they scraped the dead skin from his burns. The pain was so intense that after giving Dan all the painkillers he could take, they administered a drug that gave him amnesia for that time so he wouldn't remember the agony.

As we talked, I said, "Dan, I'm so sorry you had to go through all this."

I'll never forget his reply: "John, this has been such a rich experience. One of the richest of my life." He wasn't joking. I could see by the spark in Dan's eyes that he meant every word.

Was Dan crazy? Had there been a little too much morphine in the IV? I don't think so. I think he had discovered a life-altering secret. A hidden treasure worth far more than material wealth. A treasure I've seen lived out in many lives.

A treasure I want in my own life.

You've known people like this, too. People who refuse to be sidetracked by circumstances. People who follow Jesus through pain as well as pleasure, tragedy as well as triumph, and come through it all more invigorated and excited about life—more *passionate*—than ever before. What secret treasure do they possess?

It's not a treasure unique to today. A group of people in Ephesus discovered the same secret nearly two millennia ago.

THE WORD OF GOD

In the year A.D. 60, the city of Ephesus was one of the most important religious and cultural centers in the world. Among its three hundred thousand residents was a growing number who were cutting against the cultural grain. They had begun to believe that the one true God had come to them, died on a Roman cross, and then risen from the dead. These beliefs didn't make them very popular with those selling souvenir images of the local goddess. Competition from a new god was expected from time to time, but one man-God to whom alone *every* knee must bow? That could completely destroy business! These fanatics had to be stopped.

Despite threats from merchants and pagan rulers, members of a vibrant new church drew strength from the Lord and each other, gathering whenever they could. Then came a day when nothing could keep them apart. From every corner of this bustling port city they began to arrive. The followers of Jesus exchanged excited whispers as they looked to the leader of their young church.

"It's true," the leader said. "We have received a scroll from Paul!" It had been many months since the Ephesians had heard from Paul. But for three wonderful years he had lived with them, worked beside them, loved them, and brought them life in Christ. And so, with great anticipation, the scroll was opened. The leader began to read:

> Paul, an apostle of Christ Jesus by the will of God, to the saints in Ephesus, the faithful in Christ Jesus: Grace and peace to you from God our Father and the Lord Jesus Christ....

I picture the crowd gently leaning forward, straining to hear every word of Paul's powerful message. And what words! Paul unveils the Lord's intentions for His people as a church—to form a body expressing Christ's fullness on earth (Ephesians 1:15–23). He also reveals the ways they are to practice their saving faith—how to love their families (5:22–6:4); how to serve each other (6:7); how to fight the enemy (vv. 10–17); and how to pray (vv. 18–20).

And leaping off the scroll in the midst of it all is Paul's bold statement of faith, praise, and passion, the words found in Ephesians 3:20–21:

> Now to him who is able to do immeasurably more than all we ask or imagine, according to his power that is at work within us, to him be glory in the church and in Christ Jesus throughout all generations, for ever and ever! Amen.

As I think about the moment and the crowd of believers hanging on every word, I imagine their eyes filling with tears, for they knew something that you may have missed. Their friend Paul had written this amazing letter from prison! Paul was living out Ephesians 3:20–21 as he wrote it. Despite his desperate situation, Paul's words here—and in other prison letters like Philippians, Colossians, and 2 Timothy—are full of joy and overflowing passion.

> Rejoice in the Lord always. I will say it again: Rejoice! (Philippians 4:4)

> To this end I labor, struggling with all his energy, which so powerfully works in me. (Colossians 1:29)

> Pray also for me, that whenever I open my mouth, words may be given me so that I will fearlessly make known the mystery of the gospel, for which I am an ambassador in chains. Pray that I may declare it fearlessly, as I should. (Ephesians 6:19–20)

What incredible good news this is for us! The amazing passion Paul revealed two thousand years ago—passion that is available to us today—*cannot* be fettered. It does not stay safely behind prison bars. It invades your darkest hour, your personal dungeon. It is not hindered in the least by your circumstances. In fact, as we will see, the wonder of this faith-filling passion is that it is best displayed through impossible situations.

The Ephesians knew they were hearing something miraculous. A message had come from God's ambassador— an ambassador in chains with a chain-breaking, life-changing challenge. They must have been amazed, even overwhelmed, for they had heard and felt not only Paul's excitement and joy, but also the passion *behind* the passion—God's intense love for His children.

WALKING IN PAUL'S FOOTSTEPS

It's easy for me to picture that stirring scene in Ephesus, because a couple of years ago I walked through the ancient city myself. Traveling through Greece and Turkey to learn about the life of Paul, we all stared in wonder at the magnificence of the ruins around us. I walked the same road Paul did, past the great library of Celsus, past the shops, and even the public latrine where people sat side by side (I wondered if Paul evangelized even there!).

At one point I stopped to teach our group. We read from Paul's letter sent to the church here so long ago. We felt an awesome link to history—God's history. In the now mostly Muslim country of Turkey, I noticed that people stopped and listened, perhaps much like they did so many years ago when Paul first spoke of Jesus. Our Muslim guide, Gengis, listened carefully to all I said and afterward quietly told me, "I like the things you said about Jesus. It made me feel something in my heart. I would like to know more." I still pray for him.

From there we made our way to the great theater on the slope of Mount Pion. The acoustics were a marvel of engineering—twenty-four thousand seats, yet everyone gathered could hear perfectly.

I walked into the middle of this place, where a riot once broke out over Paul's teachings. I imagined the press of the angry mob around me. I could almost hear the deafening, idolatrous cry of the crowd. Overwhelmed in the moment, I shouted at the top of my lungs, "Jesus Christ is still Lord here!" The words echoed through the stadium and beyond as people stared.

Christ is indeed Lord there still. And He is Lord right where you are, ready to bless you with the adventure of a fully realized faith. He knows that something is missing in your life, that your heart is secretly marked by a faithless drudgery as you go about your days. He desires to change your heart in ways you've never even dreamed.

Even when Dan Cathy confronted the brushfire that threatened his life, he understood that God was in control. "I had total peace, God's peace, even out in that field with the fire burning behind me," Dan says. "I knew even then that there will never be a place I'm going to go that God is not already there."

Already there. Did you get that? The Lord is making the journey with you. In fact, He's a step in front of you, ready to lead the way to the exciting life He desires for you. Let God speak for Himself:

> I will go before you and will level the mountains; I will break down gates of bronze and cut through bars of iron. I will give you the treasures of darkness, riches stored in secret places, so that you may know that I am the LORD, the God of Israel, who summons you by name. (Isaiah 45:2–3)

Do you hear Him softly calling your name? He's not just calling you from where you are but from where you're going to be. He's saying, "Don't be afraid. I've run on ahead to tear down the walls before you arrive. There's treasure up here I want you to find. I'll do anything to keep you from living a passionless life!"

THE PASSION PROMISE

There *is* treasure waiting for you—for every believer. Most miss it because it seems so well hidden. Yet if you will only open your eyes to the Word and will of God, you'll find that the treasure chest of His very specific plan for your life is actually in plain sight. And you can unlock this incredible blessing by understanding and embracing what I call the Passion Promise:

You are designed for a life of passion—
a life only God can imagine.

In the pages ahead, we're going to clearly define the Passion Promise and then learn how to live it. I think you'll agree that if this happens in your life, the time invested reading this book will have been well spent. But let me be very clear. The treasure is not in this book. It's in *His* book.

Shall we hunt for this treasure together? Our map will be the stirring words of Ephesians 3:20–21. They led me to the treasure years ago, early in my marriage. My wonderful wife, Donna, had asked God to show her a life passage for each member of our family. She sensed God telling her that Ephesians 3:20–21 was the one for me and began using this passage as a prayer for me long before we ever talked about it. Little did I know how those words would mark and transform me.

When Donna explained what she was doing with these two verses, I began believing that this passage really was a picture of what my life was meant to be. I started to look for

God's passion experiences every day—and was overwhelmed to discover they were everywhere! I began to live in expectation instead of obligation. I no longer *had* to go to the office, or *had* to tuck in the kids, or *had* to attend that meeting. I began to see God's dream in everything. I was changed as a husband, as a father, as a pastor, as a man. My whole worldview shifted.

For as long as I could remember I had dreamed of what I could do for God. Now I saw how silly that was in the light of God's awesome dream for me!

Today, Donna and I both long to see everyone live in the passion he or she was designed for. As we seek the path to such passion in this book, my hope is that you will begin to read all of *His* book in a different way. A way that makes your heart skip a beat at the thought of what you're doing: passing through the gates of the palace, entering into the throne room, bowing at His side, trembling as the King of all kings speaks—to you! He will call your name—urgently, joyfully, tenderly. He will pull you close—so close you'll feel His breath, warm on your cheek. And then you will hear it— God's thunderous whisper—as He tells you His secrets and points to the treasure.

His Word is our map to this treasure. We can count on the accuracy of our map because we know the Word of the Lord is "a lamp to my feet and a light for my path" (Psalm 119:105). But to make the best use of this map, we'll need to examine it closely. Every word comes from God's heart and has meaning for us today. That's why we'll spend the rest of this book exploring exactly what God is telling us through these two verses.

The Ephesians were the first to be handed this amazing map. We don't know all that happened in the church at Ephesus after they read and heard these powerful words. We know that they had great impact on their city for years to come. But we also know something else. A few decades later, Jesus personally evaluated those Ephesian believers and found that they had left their passion for Him somewhere along the way:

> "I hold this against you: You have forsaken your first love. Remember the height from which you have fallen! Repent and do the things you did at first. If you do not repent, I will come to you and remove your lampstand from its place." (Revelation 2:4–5)

Sad, poignant words. But could they also describe your life? Well, the Ephesians had their shot. Now it's your turn. Make it count! Because this book is not about the people of Ephesus. They're history. It's about your chance—and your God.

The city of Ephesus is dead, but the Passion Promise lives. It's a promise that was made long ago, and a promise made for the next thirty seconds. It's a promise made…for you!

chapter two

IN THE PASSION OF
THE MOMENT

"Now..."

OULD THERE BE a more passionate word in the
English language than *now*? A young boy is with his dad on
his first big hunting trip. The gun is in his hands. His trembling finger is on the trigger. "Steady, steady, not yet. Wait on
him. *Now!*" A young bride and groom hold their breath, hop-
ing not to hear crazy Uncle Fred's voice as the minister says,
"Speak *now*, or forever hold your peace." A dying father takes
his last breath while his daughter buries her head in his chest
and whispers, "Not yet, Daddy. I need you. Don't go. Not
now."

I was interested to see the definition and sample use of
now in the *Thorndike-Barnhart Advanced Dictionary*: "adv. at

the present time; at this moment: *He is here now."*

He *is* here now! God is here in the present, calling you and me to live in the passion of the moment—*this* moment! When Paul wrote to the Ephesians, "Now to him who is able to do immeasurably more…," his use of the word *now* told his audience, "Listen up! Something important is about to happen. This moment counts."

All of us are tempted to divide our lives into "spiritual" and "regular" moments. We might expect to see God's handiwork when we're at church or when we're thinking about Him, but does God also show up at a business lunch? Does He have something to say when we're rushing to make the tuna casserole for dinner? Is He actually part of our walk from one class to another at school?

The answer is in Scripture. The Bible tells us that not one sparrow falls to the ground without God being involved (Matthew 10:29). It also says that "you are worth more than many sparrows" (v. 31). God cares about you so much that He came to earth for you, taking on human form. He lived out every minute of that life as a man. Wouldn't such a God also be concerned about every minute and second of *your* life?

Our loving God is right in the middle of your now, right where you are at this moment—and where you'll be in five minutes or five years.

Learning to think this way requires a worldview shift. Most Christians go through their whole lives as what I call "unofficial deists." Deists believe that God created the world but has little to do with it now. He certainly never supernaturally intervenes. He just made the world, wound it up, and is letting it unwind on its own.

Deism was popular in the eighteenth century, but I've never met a modern Christian who told me that he or she was a deist. In fact, I would bet that almost everyone in our churches on Sunday would categorically deny that they believe anything like this. Yet they live their lives every day as if God is not involved in each minute. Unofficially, they are deists!

"I Need a God Who Is *Here!*"

A good friend of mine developed cancer recently. He was a member of another church, but one day he told me that he and his family were joining ours. He explained why. He was listening to his pastor preach one Sunday, and the pastor said, "I certainly believe in God, but I don't believe He is actively involved in our everyday affairs." My friend said, "John, I can't stay there. I can't keep my family in that church. I have cancer. I need a God who is *here!*"

Deists can forget about experiencing the power of the Passion Promise. Because the real God is a God who is here—*now!* But do we have to get cancer to realize how desperately we need God to be active in our lives?

Our unofficial deism is often expressed in "crisis Christianity." We believe in Jesus and all that other stuff in the Bible, and we're really glad He died for us, but we don't really think much about what He's up to in our lives *now*. That is, until the walls come crashing in. Then we run to the foxhole, hunker down, and look real hard to find Him there. Because we don't know what we'll do without Him.

The amazing thing about our awesome God of love is that

He doesn't reject us during those times. He runs to meet us! But wouldn't it be incredible to know that personal power all the time? How would life change if we *really* believed in the God of the Bible—the God who is here now?

THE GOD OF NOW

Do you remember the last time you faced a real crisis and met God there? Do you recall the power of His deliverance, the depth of His comfort, the miracle of His provision? What if you could know that same power at lunch today, or when your boss gripes at you, or when you're changing a diaper? Maybe that sounds a little crazy, yet Scripture leaves no doubt that God is with us every moment of the day and paying attention to even the tiniest detail. Listen to His Word in this psalm of David:

> You know when I sit and when I rise; you perceive my thoughts from afar. You discern my going out and my lying down; you are familiar with all my ways. Before a word is on my tongue you know it completely, O LORD. You hem me in—behind and before; you have laid your hand upon me. Such knowledge is too wonderful for me, too lofty for me to attain. Where can I go from your Spirit? Where can I flee from your presence? If I go up to the heavens, you are there; if I make my bed in the depths, you are there. If I rise on the wings of the dawn, if I settle on the far side of the sea, even there your hand will guide me, your right hand will hold me fast. (Psalm 139:2–10)

Do you hear David's passion? He had discovered a God of *now*. The implications were almost too much for him. He could hardly take it all in. But he was ready to live it—and you should be, too. There's no life like it.

Understand, though, that while residing in the middle of God's passion is thrilling, it can also be frightening. God calls you to a life of moment-by-moment adventure with Him. That's exciting! But it also means that *now* matters. You can miss it. *Now* doesn't come again. And that's scary.

OLD TESTAMENT TRAGEDY

Perhaps the best and most tragic example of this in all of history was when the Israelites missed the Promised Land. They had seen God's power. They possessed God's promise. But when God said "Now!" they said "No!" And it was over. There was no going back. *Now* was gone.

They still tried to go back, though. The book of Numbers tells their story:

> Early the next morning they went up toward the high hill country. "We have sinned," they said. "We will go up to the place the LORD promised." But Moses said, "Why are you disobeying the LORD's command? This will not succeed! Do not go up, because the LORD is not with you. You will be defeated by your enemies, for the Amalekites and Canaanites will face you there. Because you have turned away from the LORD, he will not be with you and you will fall by the sword."
> Nevertheless, in their presumption they went

up toward the high hill country, though neither Moses nor the ark of the LORD's covenant moved from the camp. Then the Amalekites and Canaanites who lived in that hill country came down and attacked them and beat them down all the way to Hormah. (14:40–45)

What heartbreaking tragedy for the Israelites! Yet over my shoulder, I can see many missed "nows" of my own. I had been a follower of Jesus for only a few years when I discovered how costly it can be to miss God's "now moments."

I have always loved music, and in high school I sang in a rock band. We had a very spiritual name, "White Lightning," and we were famous—at least at a few junior high sock hops.

At practice one day, I met a guy named David who had come to "jam" with us. I ended up standing by him every day in chorus class that year. I thought he was particularly cool—he wore his hair long, was extremely popular, and appeared confident at every turn. Yet in chorus he seemed quiet, even depressed.

I began to sense God's invitation to share my faith with David. I remember wondering what he would think. Would he tell others I was strange? Would he laugh at me? As the days went by, it got easier not to say anything. I never did engage him in any way about the most important thing in my life—and the only thing that could have saved his. I had what he needed, but I kept it to myself. It was the ultimate selfishness.

I cried when I heard about David's suicide my freshman year in college. I can see his face even now, and I wonder what might have been. That "now" is gone. And missing it haunts me still.

I have missed God's promise many other times and have not been able to go back. We can't get away from the fact that God is a God of *now*. In the *New International Version* Bible, the word *now* is used almost twelve hundred times, while the word *later* appears only eighty-two times. Never does God call anyone to join him later, to follow Him later, to obey Him later. It's always *now* with God!

LATER IS TOO LATE

Most believers know this—that God is not interested in later. The bigger problem is that we try to make Him the God of "then." We make the Christian life a series of thens. *Now* we will go about our normal lives at school, at work, at home, where we assume that God isn't all that concerned about being involved. *Then* we will go to church. *Then* we will have our quiet time. *Then* God will be involved with us and we will be involved with Him.

Does this sound familiar? When we verbalize it and really think about it, that's not the way we want to live at all, is it? And yet, practically speaking, it describes the way our lives often work. But that can change for you! It must change—because *now* is the only way to live in the Passion Promise.

The Greek word for *now* in this verse is *de*. When translated *now*, in the New Testament it is often used to introduce a moment of great significance. In Matthew 5:1, *de* introduces Jesus' Sermon on the Mount. In John 11:1, it is the first word of the story about Lazarus being raised from the dead.

But *de* is not used only in relation to Jesus. The Greek *now* also introduces God's extraordinary work in the lives of seemingly ordinary people. One of them was Stephen: "*Now* Stephen, a man full of God's grace and power, did great wonders and miraculous signs among the people" (Acts 6:8). Another is Philip: "*Now* an angel of the Lord said to Philip, 'Go south to the road—the desert road—that goes down from Jerusalem to Gaza'" (8:26). That road took Philip into the power of the life-changing God.

But *now* is not always a good word to read in the Bible. It introduces Peter denying Jesus (Matthew 26:69) and Judas betraying Jesus (Mark 14:44). Yet whether used to describe good or ill, *now* is always momentous. That's why God, through Paul, chose to begin one of His most important messages—Ephesians 3:20–21—with a word that conveys great significance.

A life of significance, fully experienced in every moment, is exactly what God is calling you to. It is a life of passion.

HOW NOW?

So what do you do *now*? That's a critical question, and it will require this whole book to answer it. I encourage you to be patient with yourself—right now! That may sound like a contradiction, but it's a necessary one.

You are about to make a major life change. You are going to grasp the amazing reality of the adventure God meant the Christian life to be. It's a lot to take in. At first you may even find yourself a little depressed as you think about all you've missed trying to live your life apart from the passion of God's heart. Don't become discouraged. You'll discover plenty of excitement in the days ahead—in fact, for all eternity.

But let's not waste time getting started. Get ready to dive into some deep, mysterious, and wonderful waters. If you're just learning to swim, that's all right. You may find yourself thrashing around and making little progress, but just when you think you may sink, you'll realize that God's just taking you deeper into His passion. And He can't wait to show you all that's under the surface.

For a scuba diver, there's no better place on earth to go under the surface than Punta Sur, a famous dive site off the Mexican island of Cozumel in the Caribbean. I had read and dreamed about it for years before I finally had the chance to dive it.

The dive guide led us through incredibly clear water down to the entrance of a cave in the reef. I went vertical and descended into the darkness. Clicking on my flashlight, I saw small colorful fish darting between multihued coral formations. I cleared the pressure from my ears as we dropped down—70, 80, 100, 120, 130 feet.

Suddenly the tunnel turned and opened into the impossibly blue depth of the Caribbean. It was a sheer cliff wall. I peered over the edge, and below me I could see nothing but blue for hundreds of feet—straight down. Above me I could see the waves breaking on the surface. They seemed very far away. The cliff wall was covered with living coral of every color of the rainbow. It was beauty beyond belief, beyond words.

I wanted to see more. I swam out of the cave—*over the edge*. It's scary to swim over the edge, but in scuba diving, that's where the real adventure begins. That's what you're there for. But there is danger over the edge as well.

Entranced by the beauty of it all, I made a mistake. Not an uncommon mistake, but at this depth a dangerous one. While taking in the magnificent scenery, I lost track of my buddies and my depth.

That's when it happened—what divers know as nitrogen narcosis. I was trained for it, had even experienced a little of it before, but I had never felt anything like this.

I had let myself drift down too far—below 145 feet. Narcosis, or being "narced," robs you of your common sense. Everything slows down. You feel like you're in a fog, and you may not make wise decisions. Make the wrong one and you may not live to make another.

When I realized that I was way too deep and alone, I felt the cold chill of nitrogen-induced confusion. I wasn't so much in a panic; I just wasn't sure what to do now.

Now! That's it!

My training began to kick in. Years before, my instructor had taught me that if I was ever narced, I should stop and ask myself, *What is the one thing that I am to do* right now? In that bewildering and dangerous moment, I forced myself to think...and then I knew. *I must slowly ascend.* I did just that— safely.

Close call. Incredible adventure.

Yet my adventure at Punta Sur doesn't come close to the adventure of experiencing a passionate life designed by God. God is calling each of us over the edge. It's scary out there, yes. It's not even completely safe. But over the edge is where you'll find the wonder and glory and beauty of the life God has for you.

Will you answer His call? Will you go deeper into real life? You don't have to, you know. He won't make you. There's a reason why God so often says in Scripture that we are not to reject His call. He leaves the decision entirely up to us. He can call you to a journey of change, yet you can choose to stay home. He can call you to serve someone else, and you can serve yourself instead. He can call you over the edge, and you can carefully turn back toward safe ground. But you've already been there, haven't you?

Come on, let's answer His call. Let's go somewhere we've *never* been! Over the edge—where He is *now*. And when you feel narced, when the fog seems to settle in, remember one thing. God is whispering to you, "What is it you need to do *right now*? You know what it is because I'm with you, teaching you. Just do *right now* what you know I'm calling you to—and I will be there. Always."

What's the one thing you need to do right now? Let's find out.

chapter three

CHOOSE YOUR PASSION

"To him who is able..."

HOOSE YOUR PASSION.

That's the one thing. The one thing to do right now. The one thing that will mean everything in your life. Make no mistake about this choice, because choosing the wrong passion will destroy you and choosing no passion will deplete you.

Passion is a dangerous commodity. Misplaced passion leads men and women to trade their souls for a few more dollars or to trade their families for ten minutes of sex. Self-centered theological passion can result in the cheap gospel of health and wealth: *If I just love Jesus, there will always be more stuff for me!* Prideful passion is nothing more than ego-driven ambition that never satisfies.

Ask King David what happens when a man after God's heart decides to follow his own heart—*his* passion. Adultery, murder, death, and discipline.

Ask Peter about prideful passion: "Not me, Jesus. I'll never deny you!" Shame, grief, and defeat.

Ask Judas where a passion for money and personal power leads. Betrayal, suicide, hell itself.

And if your passion is for a misguided image of God, you will not only be wrong—you'll become an instrument of evil. Some extremely passionate men flew airplanes into buildings on September 11.

So this choice means just about everything to you and me. If we determine that we will not live passionless lives, that we will live for something, even die for it if necessary, how do we choose the *right* passion? How do we ensure that our choice will lead to adventure instead of disaster?

The *source* of our passion is the key.

A GREAT PROMISE

To him who is able...

Those are simple, profound, life-giving words! God claims that He is *able*, completely capable of doing what He says He will do. Ephesians 3:20–21 is the foundation of the Passion Promise, but the phrase "To him who is able" actually qualifies these two verses as a promise in themselves.

Theologians call Ephesians 3:20–21 a doxology. A doxology is a passage of Scripture that ascribes praise and glory to God. Paul praises God because "He is able." The Scripture leaves absolutely no doubt about God's ability.

Renowned Greek scholar A. T. Robertson points out that a doxology can be a promise as well. He says of this passage, "The doxology ascribes to God the power to do them [the things He promises] for us."[1] Then there is *The Complete Biblical Library*, one of the most comprehensive study tools ever produced. It describes this passage as "a great promise."[2] These two verses are, in fact, a guarantee that God has great plans for our lives, that He can deliver on those plans, and that His intentions are far beyond anything we could accomplish or hope for on our own.

Of course, Ephesians 3:20–21 isn't the only passage in Scripture that calls the believer to a life of passion. But nothing is more powerful than the simple statement that "He is able." Period. He waits today to see if you will believe it…and if you will *choose* to live it out every day.

Two of Jesus' disciples, James and John, once came to have a talk with Jesus. Matthew tells us they brought Mom along to help bolster their position. After all, they were asking for great places of honor with Jesus when He came into His glory. Who better than their mother to make their case?

Jesus, knowing the price He would pay before He entered glory, asked them, "Are you able to drink the cup that I drink, and be baptized with the baptism that I am baptized with?" (Mark 10:38, NKJV). They answered, "We *are able*," (v. 39)—using the same Greek word we find in Ephesians 3:20.

Were they able? Were they capable of achieving that dream? Not even close! They were clueless. Jesus told them they didn't even know what they were asking.

Where did they miss it? What was their problem? The

exact same problem you and I face when we choose our source of passion. As long as we think *we* are able, we will never experience what it means to know that *He* is able!

Interestingly, Jesus told these two power-seekers that one day they *would* be able to follow Him. They would suffer as He did. They would know power and adventure and glory and passion. But to get there they had to fail, to come to the end of themselves, to see that they were not able at all. It was then that they would be ready for the second chapter of Acts—for the fire and wind of heaven to explode into their very being, filling them with the One who alone is able!

That was the only source of genuine passion for them. It's still the only one for you, too.

WHO IS HE, ANYWAY?

If we are going to believe that He is able, we better have an accurate idea of who *He* is! It's frightening how little the unchurched world knows about the God of the Bible.

I often send a team of video guys from our church out into our community to do Jay Leno–style street interviews. Every time we show these interviews to the congregation, we realize that not only do most people not know God, they don't even know who He is! They view Him as a boring, grandfatherly rule-maker or an ethereal, all-encompassing force—or whatever they need Him to be that day. But they know little or nothing about Jesus and what He taught.

In our most recent interviews, we asked Atlanta residents living right in the middle of the Bible Belt if they knew who said "You must be born again." One guy confidently answered, "Thomas Jefferson." Some had no clue. One thought it was a rock star. One, at least, chose a biblical figure: "Simon Peter."

What's even scarier, though, is that the church doesn't seem to know God much better. It seems to me that the vast majority of the people in our churches view God as the one who is supposed to take care of us—they believe that's His primary nature. So when we're sick, He's there to make us well. When we have a problem, He's there to straighten it out. When we're bad, He's there to help us be better. We want to sing the songs we like, hear the sermons we like, and do things the way we like—because God is supposed to take good care of us.

OUR PASSIONATE GOD

Now, I'm not saying that God doesn't meet the real needs of His people, but aren't you interested in a God who is more than a babysitter? The God of the Bible cares deeply about everything! He created the world with infinite and indescribable passion.

The first time the Bible says that God was angry is in Exodus 4:14. What upset Him so much? Moses, his chosen servant, basically said, "Get someone else, Lord." God is passionately angry when we risk missing His best for us!

God is passionate in His sorrow. When He sent His Son to the world, He had already told us that He would be "a man of sorrows" (Isaiah 53:3). And at that soul-wrenching, history-changing appointment in Gethsemane, Jesus told His best friends that His soul was "overwhelmed with sorrow to the point of death" (Matthew 26:38).

God is passionate in His joy. The first time in the Bible that the phrase "the joy of the Lord" is used, it makes clear that its purpose is not to make us feel better but to fill us with power. Nehemiah says, "The joy of the LORD is your *strength*" (8:10). God's joy is power. God's joy is passion.

God is passionate in His love. Paul wrote, "But God demonstrates His own love for us in this: While we were still sinners, Christ died for us" (Romans 5:8). Enough said!

God is passionate in *all* He does. He is quite capable of meeting your needs, but He longs for you to go way beyond that and share His life. Hebrews 12:29 says, "Our God is a consuming fire." And in Romans 12:11, Paul says, "Never be lacking in zeal, but keep your spiritual fervor, serving the Lord."

The Greek word for "spiritual fervor" is the best one-word definition of the heart of God and of the message of the Passion Promise. The word literally means "to boil or to be fervent." The *Complete Biblical Library* says it means "to be ardent in boiling over with holy enthusiasm."[3] That's the heart of God, and that's how the Bible says we are to serve Him.

Instead of praying for God to bless us, what if this Sunday your pastor asked God to "burn us up and boil us over"? That's a prayer God would love to hear! That reflects who He really is.

Jesus makes it clear that it's serious business to Him if we reject His heart of passion and choose a life of lukewarmness. In fact, Jesus says that when we live this way, it makes Him want to throw up (Revelation 3:16). The answer to this, according to Jesus, is to "be earnest [or fervent], and repent"

(v. 19). So according to Jesus, we can live in His passion or in His vomit. It's our choice.

GETTING IN GOD'S FACE

No matter where you go in the Bible, you can't get away from our Lord's true nature—a God of power and passion who calls you to know Him as the One "who is able." At the Last Supper, when Philip asked Jesus to "show us the Father" (John 14:8), Jesus chastised him: "Don't you believe that I am in the Father, and that the Father is in me?... It is the Father, living in me, who is doing his work" (v. 10).

It's all over the Old Testament, too. One of my favorite Bible characters is Hezekiah, a man filled with passion for God. A man who understood who God was in a day when few others did—and who found out firsthand that God is able.

Hezekiah was a young, radical king of Judah seven hundred years before Christ. He was a bold leader who smashed the idols of his people and led them to worship God alone. He even smashed the bronze serpent Moses had made, which had become an idol (2 Kings 18:4). Hezekiah probably wouldn't have made it a month as a pastor of most churches today. Too much passion!

Hezekiah rebelled against a king named Sennacherib, who had already destroyed forty-six cities. Sennacherib was 46-0, and he was coming for Jerusalem and for the young ruler. Hezekiah knew that there was no way he could win. So he did the one thing he could do—he turned to the One who *was* able.

In 2 Kings 19:15–19, Hezekiah prayed one of the greatest prayers in the Bible. In fact, it is so incredible that it is repeated word for word in Isaiah 37. Hezekiah went up to the temple and spread out the letter from Sennacherib for the Lord to see. As you read Hezekiah's prayer, imagine you are there, listening to every word. Feel Hezekiah's passion for the only One able to save his people:

> "O LORD, God of Israel, enthroned between the cherubim, you alone are God over all the kingdoms of the earth.... Give ear, O LORD, and hear; open your eyes, O LORD, and see; listen to the words Sennacherib has sent to insult the living God.
>
> "It is true, O LORD, that the Assyrian kings have laid waste these nations and their lands. They have thrown their gods into the fire and destroyed them, for they were not gods but only wood and stone, fashioned by men's hands. Now, O LORD, our God, deliver us from his hand, so that all kingdoms on earth may know that you alone, O LORD, are God."

Now that's a passion prayer. Hezekiah got in God's face! He said in essence, "Can't You hear, God? You're not blind, are You? Look at what this man is doing!" If I used those words with God, I'd be watching for lightning bolts.

But Hezekiah could talk to God that way because he knew Him—intimately. Hezekiah understood who God was and that His honor was at stake. He turned from his own ability and completely trusted God's. That's spiritual fervor boiling over.

In response, God told Hezekiah that Sennacherib would not lay a hand on Jerusalem. And He kept His promise, as the defeated king ran from the angel of God back to his home, where he was killed by his own sons. How did all this come about? "The *passion* of the LORD Almighty will make this happen!" (2 Kings 19:31, NLT).

By the way, when God told us He would send His own Son, He said the same thing: "The passionate commitment of the LORD Almighty will guarantee this!" (Isaiah 9:7, NLT). Are you starting to see it? The power of a life lived not in your ability but in His?

That's the "one thing"—the source of real passion.

CHOOSING THE ONE THING OVER THE OTHER THINGS

If anything amazes God, it must be that we can see His power and passion—and choose counterfeits instead. Because more often than not, that is exactly what we do.

Each of my children ate weird things when they were small. When my son Trey learned to crawl, he crawled everywhere! One day my wife Donna and I "misplaced" him and went on a frantic search. My heart skipped a beat when I saw that the door to the garage was cracked open. Not a good place for a little guy to hang out. I held my breath and opened the door, and sure enough, there he was—in front of the dog food bowl, having himself a little snack. Alpo from head to toe!

My daughter Amy had a fondness for poison. If we turned around for a second she grabbed something deadly

and consumed it. We became good friends with the Poison
Control folks. One day while Donna was polishing the dining
room table, Amy sneaked up behind her and slugged down
the furniture polish. She didn't suffer any permanent consequences, but she had lemon-fresh breath for days.

My oldest daughter, Christi, doesn't care for fishing now,
but when she was small she loved to go with Daddy to the
lake. One day I sat her down to play, baited a catfish line with
a big Canadian night crawler, and then started walking along
the bank fishing for bass. Looking back to check on Christi,
I could hardly believe my eyes. She had one of those big old
worms hanging out of the corner of her mouth! I ran toward
her but it was too late.

Have you ever seen someone eat pasta? Christi sucked
that worm down whole and then gave me the sweetest smile.
I told her mommy about it—a few years later.

What is it with my children? I would have given them
any good thing to eat that they wanted, but they chose dog
food, poison, and worms! The rest of us aren't so different,
though. We're God's children, but we often just don't get it.
We crawl around in our immaturity, eating whatever we find
because we haven't yet grown up enough to be filled with the
One who is *able*!

C. S. Lewis said it like this: "We are half-hearted crea-
tures, fooling about with drink and sex and ambition when
infinite joy is offered to us, like an ignorant child who wants
to go on making mud pies in the slum because he cannot
imagine what is meant by the offer of a holiday at the sea."[4]

Our problem is that we have spent so much time in the
mud that "mud pies"—fleeting pleasures such as new homes

and cars, extramarital affairs, and fame and fortune—look good to us.

But you have to choose. Jesus said that "no one can serve two masters" (Matthew 6:24). So the simple fact is that you will either choose to drift through life without purpose, pursuing whatever appears enticing at the moment as your passion, or you will choose the One who is able—the only One who is able—as your source of true passion.

The big question you have to answer is: "What do you really want from life?" The amazing thing is that *God* asks you the question! God invited Solomon to ask Him for whatever he wanted. Rather than choosing the obvious requests of riches and power, Solomon answered, "Give your servant a discerning heart to govern your people and to distinguish between right and wrong" (1 Kings 3:9). God gave Solomon exactly what he asked for and more.

I know what you're thinking: *God asked Solomon that question, not me!* But listen to what Jesus says to *all* His followers: "Ask and it will be given to you; seek and you will find; knock and the door will be opened to you. For everyone who asks receives; he who seeks finds; and to him who knocks, the door will be opened" (Matthew 7:7–8).

So what will you ask for? What will be your passion? More important, *who* will be your passion?

THE PASSION PARADOX

The dictionary says that a paradox is "a statement that may be true though it seems to be false." Here is the passion paradox: *You can't find passion by seeking it.*

That doesn't seem to make sense, does it? But if you look at our society, you'll see the truth of it everywhere. For generations people have sought passion by pursuing every kind of pleasure. Even though we know that drugs and alcohol destroy lives, that sexual promiscuity can become addictive and lead to deadly diseases, and that people with ridiculous amounts of money can still become so depressed they don't want to live, we seem to think that we'll be the exception. Somehow we'll find the passion that everyone else has missed in all that stuff.

But it never happens! It just doesn't work that way. Genuine passion is only found in the heart of the One who created it—the Creator of everything. To know that passion, you must find it in His heart. The beauty of this paradox is that you can have passion when you have nothing else at all.

Psalm 63 is a great passion passage. In this psalm you meet David when he has lost just about all there is to lose. He has borne the consequences of serious sin; he has lost his throne; his wealth is gone; he is homeless; his own son is trying to kill him. That's bad!

Facing all of this, what is David's response? Despair? Hopelessness? No way! He knows where his passion comes from. "O God, you are my God, earnestly I seek you; my soul thirsts for you, my body longs for you, in a dry and weary land where there is no water" (v. 1). He isn't seeking his possessions or his kingdom; he is seeking the King! And that is enough for him: "Because your love is better than life, my lips will glorify you" (v. 3).

That's the passion paradox. Chase passion and you'll never catch it. Chase the Creator and you'll find passion everywhere!

A PERSON OF AUTHENTIC PASSION

So let's clearly define what you're after—this passion you can choose. The one thing. To live out this passion, to give your life entirely *to Him who is able*—how will you live?

I believe that there are four keys to discovering the authentic life of passion God has designed for you. You must:

- FOCUS ON THE CREATOR—God is the Author of passion. Only when you spend time daily in worship, in prayer, and in His Word will you develop a close relationship with Him and begin to fully experience the passionate life He has designed for you.
- REJECT IMITATIONS—We are continually bombarded with distractions that claim to offer authentic passion, whether it is career ambition, the pursuit of wealth, illicit sex and pornography, or drugs. All are short-term "fixes" that fall pitifully short of the thrill of fulfilling God's purpose for your life.
- ALWAYS EXPECT JOYFUL PASSION—God loves you passionately and has imagined an incredible life for you! When you rely on Him daily, He can lead you into a life of joy and excitement beyond anything you have envisioned.
- INTENTIONALLY SHARE GENUINE PASSION—When you spread the joy of an authentic, passionate life in God to others, it brings further glory to God, and it increases your own joy when, like the image in a mirror, it is reflected back to you.

Think deeply about these keys. Memorize them. This really can be your life! As you pursue God and the passionate life, however, realize that everything in our world will try to call you away from Him.

THE GREAT GRAPE JELLY MYSTERY

The winds of Desert Storm were blowing, and Colonel William Post had a job to do. He was in charge of receiving all of the incoming supplies for the ground forces. Among these supplies were the tons of food that came in every day.

One day Colonel Post received a message from the Pentagon requesting that he account for forty cases of missing grape jelly. The Colonel sent a soldier to investigate the mysterious missing jelly; the solider reported back that it couldn't be found. Colonel Post made his report and assumed that would be the end of it. After all, it was just grape jelly.

He assumed wrong. The Pentagon continued to press him, pointing out that they needed to close the books for the month, and jelly just couldn't vanish like that. Finally they *ordered* him to find the jelly!

The Colonel had had enough by then and sent back this response: "Sirs, you must decide. I can dispatch the entire army to find your missing jelly *or* kick Saddam out of Kuwait, but not both!" He got no reply.

I was asked to speak to the Georgia State House of Representatives and told this story. I thought it was pretty funny and expected to get quite a laugh out of it. However, much to my dismay, when I got to the punch line, I was greeted by a roomful of blank stares! I later asked one of the representatives, a friend of mine, what in the world had gone wrong. He smiled and said, "John, you were speaking to a bunch of bureaucrats. They're still wondering where that jelly is! As soon as you leave, someone will probably make a motion that we keep trying to find it."

I have a jar of grape jelly sitting on my desk. I like grape jelly. This jar is *homemade* jelly! The best kind. But I'll never eat it. It will sit there until Jesus returns. It reminds me that there are countless things in this world that look good to me. Some of them even *are* good. But they're just grape jelly! They are not worthy to be my passion or my master. I don't have time to search for them and neither do you.

Life is short. While we run down the road on a jelly search, the One who is able is here right now. Right in front of us. And He is the source of genuine passion. The *only* source.

Are you hungry for some jelly? Then put down this book and go on your way. *Your* way. But if your choice is Jesus, the Author of passion, to be your very life, well, then, let's continue on our journey together!

chapter four

MEASURE YOUR PASSION

"To do immeasurably more..."

WHEN I TURNED FORTY, I went to the Cooper Clinic in Dallas for a comprehensive physical exam. The first task of this thoroughly humiliating day was to be weighed and measured. I stood on the scales and heard myself pronounced 190 pounds and five feet nine inches.

I immediately informed the technician that there had to be some mistake. One hundred ninety pounds I could believe, but I had been five-ten since high school! All day long the staff at the clinic tested me for everything from cancer to diabetes to heart disease, but what really worried me was where that lost inch had gone.

At the end of the day my doctor looked at all my test

results and proclaimed me to be in fine health. I said, "I appreciate that, but now I'd very much like to know why I'm shrinking!" After I further explained myself, the doctor informed me that there was a perfectly logical explanation. Since I had always been involved in sports, over the years my joints had compressed, robbing me of a little of my height. And worse, she said that by the time I was fifty-five I would probably lose another inch. I really was shrinking!

Later I told this story at church, and the congregation enjoyed it. At lunch that day, my son, Trey, then nine, was intrigued by all this. He asked, "Dad, is it true that the older you get the shorter you get?" I said, "I guess so, son." After a thoughtful pause, he said with all seriousness, "That Methuselah [the oldest man who ever lived] must have been one short dude!"

It is amazing that the God who created everything with His word and set us free by personally assaulting death itself should have followers like us who settle for shriveled-up, pint-size passions. We may not be able to stop ourselves from shrinking, but we can choose for our passion to be as big as God's.

Yet how do you know if your passion is God-sized? How do you measure this? If you have chosen Jesus as your life and you want to be a person of authentic passion, how do you evaluate your passion to be sure you're not slipping back into the smallness of your own desires?

One thing is sure—typical measures of success will not identify God-sized passion. Our churches are full of people who come when it's convenient, because they know they are supposed to, or because they want to feel better. They never have a clue about the real adventure God has for them.

These are people who measure the significance of their life in exactly the same way unbelievers do—by their income, their career success, and the size of their toy box. But that never has worked! Why would any Christian want his or her life to be measured by the world's standards?

A. W. Tozer writes, "The average person in the world today, without faith and without hope, is engaged in a desperate personal search throughout his lifetime. He does not really know where he has been. He does not really know what he is doing here and now. He does not know where he is going. The sad commentary is that he is doing it all on borrowed time and borrowed money and borrowed strength—and he already knows that in the end he will surely die."[5]

Tozer is right, isn't he? He nailed it. You know people just like that; they don't even see their need for something more. But no Christian ought to live this way. What a phenomenal waste of the resources right in front of us.

Compared to anything else you seek, God is able to do "immeasurably more" in your life. The phrase means "above the greatest abundance." Remember—a person of authentic passion *focuses on the Creator of passion.* So God's passion in us will always be God-sized!

I have a friend in the former Soviet Union named Constantin, who went through terrible suffering as a pastor under Communism. Every pastor of the church before him had been executed. Not a lot of résumés in the stack for that pastoral search team!

My friend survived, but spent seven years in Siberian labor camps for the crime of teaching children the Good News of Jesus instead of the Communist party line. He was constantly cold, away from his family, lonely, and human. He told me that sometimes he would pray that God would let him die so he could leave the suffering and be with Jesus. Even now, every time I go see him, I bring medicine for the horrible pain in his hands from the cold and labor he endured.

One day I said to Constantin, "What is your secret? How did you face all this and still find purpose and passion in your life? I want to tell American believers your answer." He simply said, "Tell my American brothers and sisters that Jesus is enough."

Case closed! Don't settle for the world's imitations and substitutions. A person of authentic passion just can't do it. He *rejects imitations*. Only God's passion is enough.

THE PASSION TEST

Are there practical ways to evaluate whether you're really living all the life God has for you? Yes! Use three questions as your "passion test." Why these particular questions? Because I have never met anyone who could answer yes to all three who was not experiencing God's "immeasurable" passion.

1. Are you actively exploring the love of God?
2. Are you developing passionate relationships?
3. Are you running *toward* the impossible?

If your Christian life consists of trying to keep God's rules, you will never understand God at all. Though it doesn't make any sense, He is consumed with love for you! You may go through such terrible trials that you don't always feel loved, but the Cross is the ultimate proof of His love. John 3:16 hasn't changed: "For God *so loved* the world that he gave his one and only Son."

God is absolutely passionate about you. And He invites you to explore the full wonder and mystery of that fervent love. Every day! That can be your life. A person of authentic passion *always expects joyful passion.*

Listen to God's heart: "Call to me and I will answer you and tell you great and unsearchable things you do not know" (Jeremiah 33:3). What an invitation! Fast-forward several hundred years and hear from Paul: "No eye has seen, no ear has heard, no mind has conceived what God has prepared for those who love him" (1 Corinthians 2:9). Jesus sums it up: "I have come that they may have life, and have it to the full" (John 10:10).

Life to the full! But you can never know a fraction of the life He has for you unless you actively explore the love of God: "As the Father has loved me, so have I loved you. Now remain in my love" (John 15:9). Tender, impossibly wonderful words. And every day that you don't step deeper into that love is a day in which you miss the passionate life God imagines for you.

We've been talking about the phrase "to do immeasurably more" from Ephesians 3:20. You only need to go back three verses to see how God wants you to measure passion: "And I pray that you, being rooted and established in *love*, may have power, together with all the saints, to grasp how wide and long and high and deep is the *love* of Christ, and to know this *love* that surpasses knowledge—that you may be filled to the measure of all the fullness of God" (vv. 17–19).

Wow! Now that's love. Love that so surpasses knowledge

you can never fully take it in. God invites us to dive ever deeper into that love for the rest of our lives.

Is the love of God wider and longer and higher and deeper in your life today than yesterday? That's how to evaluate your passion. Jesus said it Himself: "'Love the Lord your God with all your heart and with all your soul and with all your mind.' This is the first and greatest commandment" (Matthew 22:37–38). Sounds pretty passionate to me.

Don't make the mistake of thinking that exploring the love of God is only some ethereal, mystical experience. The love of God is written down for you on paper, there in His Word for you to experience every day. We meet God and His love in the Bible. The reason many people struggle to read the Bible regularly is that they never really expect the love they find there to come off the page and invade their life. But that's how God works.

Try this. Begin asking God to work supernaturally to bring to life in real, visible ways what you are reading in His Word. Get ready, though, because once you see that God really works this way, you'll never be able to go back to life as "normal." You will start looking for the Word of God to come alive around every corner!

Once you've done that, try something even more exciting. Ask God to do this in the lives of those you love. Ask out loud so they can hear it. God loves this kind of faith.

MISSIONARY MAGIC

I took my eleven-year-old son, Trey, on a mission trip to Uganda last year. My wife and I prayed that God would use this time to teach Trey how He works. In fact, we prayed out loud over him that God would show Trey His power so clearly that he couldn't miss it and would never doubt the awesome adventure God has in mind for him.

But from the beginning of our trip, everything seemed to go wrong. One of our team lost her passport and was left behind. The planes were delayed and we ended up stuck in London. We were tired and discouraged as we woke up in the hotel and prepared to go to the airport to try to get to Africa.

My wife, Donna, had written notes for Trey and me to read with a Scripture passage each day. For that first day she had written down Psalm 91. This was Donna's and my life passage for Trey. He almost died at birth, and the last thing Donna said to me before going under anesthesia for an emergency C-section was "Read Psalm 91!" So this was already a powerful passage for us. Trey and I asked God to bring it alive in our lives that day.

As we got on the elevator to go down to the hotel lobby, a tall black man joined us. As we stood silently in the elevator, suddenly, to our amazement, the man began to sing, "He who dwells in the shelter of the Most High will rest in the shadow of the Almighty! I will say of the Lord, He is my refuge and my fortress, my God, in whom I trust!"

"You're singing Psalm 91!" I said.

"Yes," he said with a smile and walked off the elevator. My son's eyes were glued wide open. We shared this with all our group, went to the airport with joy, and landed safely in Uganda. As we began to exit the plane, to our disbelief a man at the front of the plane turned and shouted, "May the blessings of God rest on all those who do His work here!"

Same guy! On our plane! But why should we be surprised that the God who loves us so much would work this way to show a young boy His power? And He wasn't through yet.

I had told Trey that if he wanted to go with me on the mission trip, he had to have a mission of his own. He likes to do magic tricks, so we decided that he would be the missionary magician. We worked out a way for him to share the gospel using his tricks. He would make things disappear and say, "Jesus will make your sins disappear." We figured he might do his tricks for some kids on the street or for a Sunday school class at the church.

I was there to preach at a crusade in a soccer stadium. On the first night, after I preached, I was surprised that so few people wanted to talk to me. I had preached at overseas crusades many times, and people always gathered after we finished. Then I noticed that a huge crowd had surrounded my son at the other end of the stadium. They weren't interested in talking to me because they wanted to see the "magic boy"!

When I finally worked my way through the crowd to my son, he said, "Daddy, get me out of here!" We ran for the bus with a throng of my son's fans chasing us. The next day he was asked to do his magic for eight hundred children at a school. Then on Sunday many of those same children came to church, where my son shared the gospel and led hundreds of them to Christ.

One major problem developed, though. The leaders of the church told me that the people thought my son was a witch doctor! The witch doctors of that area also used tricks to gain control of the people. So on the last night of the crusade, my son stood before the whole crowd and showed them one of his secrets. The people gasped in amazement when Trey pulled his "thumb" off—and then showed them it was actually a plastic thumb. He said, "See, this is just a trick. Only Jesus has real power!"

Church leaders told us that with that one simple demonstration, the witch doctors lost their control over the people. God had used an eleven-year-old boy to help break the power of darkness over a whole city. Do you think Trey will ever forget that? Do you think his dad will? I'd say that a father and son will remember for the rest of their lives the power and love of God they saw together on the other side of the world.

And on your side of the world, *you* have the privilege of exploring the awesome love of God and looking for it to come alive all around you.

PASSION PARTNERS

When you begin to keep the love of God to yourself, it ceases to be the love of God. God's love was made to be shared. Jesus said that a second great commandment flows from the first— "Love your neighbor as yourself" (Matthew 22:39).

A person of authentic passion *intentionally shares genuine passion*.

The phrase "immeasurably more" from Ephesians 3:20 is never translated that way again in the Bible. But it is used two other times. Both are in 1 Thessalonians, and both are used to describe Paul's passion for relationship. In 1 Thessalonians 3:10, Paul says, "Night and day we pray *most earnestly* that we may see you again." Paul longed to share his passion with those who understood it and lived it as he did.

You can give up on the idea of living the life God intends for you if your faith consists of sitting anonymously in church on Sundays. You need passion partners! If you're married, live out the Passion Promise with your spouse. Talk about it, watch what God does, and celebrate it. And everyone needs passionate friends—partners in life who have each other's backs, who are headed in the same direction, and who can't wait to see what the next day with Jesus holds.

I see His passion in the eyes of my own friends. I know it better because I see it lived out in them. I hear it on the phone in the voices of my friends Doug and Alvin, who live far away but are always living where God is working. I see it in my friend Woody's eyes, his passion for what God is doing in the men of our church, as hundreds gather at 5:45 every Monday morning to learn together how to be real men. I see it in Rich's eyes as he stands amazed at how God has used him, a Delta Airlines pilot, to launch our missions ministry all over the world. I see it in my crazy friend Dave's eyes as God uses his humor to bring joy and Jesus to others. I see it in Stan's eyes as he dreams God's dreams, bigger than what most people think about even once in their lives.

Pursue depth in your relationships. Take an honest look at your friendships. Are they primarily that of casual buddies whose conversations never go beyond golf scores? Or long phone calls that extensively cover everyone else's life but never really address the issues of your own? It's important to be able to see passion deepen in your friends' lives over the long journey. Having the accountability and comradeship of a best friend like I have with my friend Doug is critical to sustaining lifelong passion. You need people in your life who will always be there to encourage you, but will also kick you in the rear when you're about to make a mess of things. Friends like that are passion partners!

I encourage everyone on our church staff to have a mentor—someone who is a little farther down the road in an area where they want to grow. My good friend Crawford Lorritts plays that role in my life now. Both of us have hectic schedules, and we don't really get that much time together, but when we finally pull aside to talk, God speaks to me personally.

Crawford always seems to have encouragement for me from God's Word at just the right time. A while ago I was pretty discouraged—almost passionless actually. Crawford and I met and he wanted to take me to Leviticus 24.

Oh boy. Leviticus, I thought. I couldn't think of even one verse I'd ever memorized from Leviticus. Well, I can now! Chapter 24 begins, "The LORD said to Moses, 'Command the Israelites to bring you clear oil of pressed olives for the light so that the lamps may be kept burning continually.'"

"Sometimes, John," Crawford told me, "you have to be pressed hard before God can bring from your life the clearest oil that will burn the brightest." I'll never forget it. What a friend! A passion partner.

We don't have to be in this alone. We're not meant to be. I'm blessed to see God's passion in the eyes of more friends than I can name. But even if you have only one partner—just one friend who really believes this wild stuff about a God who gives life beyond imagination—then that's enough, and more than the vast majority of people will ever have.

Find that person! He or she is out there looking for you, too. Then go live out His passion as you see it reflected in the eyes of that friend.

COMFORT OR THE CROSS?

When I first came to pastor New Hope Baptist Church in Fayetteville, Georgia, a little boy named Zach would come to talk to me almost every Sunday. He was always full of fire and ready to conquer the universe. One day he said, "Pastor John, I'm gonna be a preacher when I grow up!"

"That's wonderful, Zach!" I said.

"Yeah, and I'll be the pastor of New Hope after you're dead."

He just might be! He's a member of our youth group now and still believes that God can use him to touch the world. I think God relishes that kind of passion from a child or an adult. He doesn't care about age. He's just looking for those who aren't afraid of the big challenge, of what everyone says can't be done—of the impossible.

It's easy to recognize Christians who are missing the Passion Promise. They are the ones who spend their lives trying to stay as comfortable as possible. Most of the divisions in churches result from desperate efforts to stay comfortable— to get our way. We want to sing our kind of songs with our kind of people, led by our kind of pastor, in our kind of church. We just want to be comfortable. But you really can't follow Jesus that way. There's just not much comfort in taking up a cross!

The Crucifixion was the most impossible situation in history. How could anything good come of something so horrible? And yet from the cross came every good thing we have and are. The Passion Promise is most clearly seen in all its wonder in the midst of impossible situations. If you spend your whole life running from what you can't handle, you will never see God do what only He can handle.

One of the strangest things about measuring your passion is that you can be sure you're on target when you start to look forward to impossible situations and run *to* them instead of *from* them—not because you enjoy difficulties, but because it's such a kick to see how God solves them. Every time God overcomes the "impossible," it builds up the faith of everyone involved and brings glory to Him.

Another form of the phrase "immeasurably more" is found in 2 Corinthians 7. Paul talks about all the troubles he and his friends were facing—exhaustion, conflict, fear. They were "harassed at every turn." But in the midst of all this, he says, "My joy *knows no bounds*" (v. 4). He could not measure his joy by earthly standards because he had met God in the middle of the impossible. You can, too!

VICTORIA'S MIRACLE

A few years ago my wife prayed that God would "expand her territory" and allow her to be a part of impossible situations that only He could handle. My brother Michael, a pediatric intensive care specialist, called in the middle of her prayer time. He told Donna an amazing story.

Michael had been contacted about a baby who was dying

on the other side of the world, in a West African country called the Gambia. Her parents, Lazarus and Joy, were missionaries from Nigeria, and their baby, Victoria, had been born with serious health problems. The doctors told Lazarus that the baby would die and not even to tell his wife she was alive at birth. The doctors would not feed her, and Lazarus got grave clothes ready and dug a grave. But the little girl wouldn't die! Critically ill and starving, she clung to life.

After several days, believing that some miracle was taking place, Lazarus contacted someone in America who knew my brother. My brother began working to see if there was any way to get the baby to America. There was no money, no visas, no answers, and almost no time. So why, my wife wondered, was my brother calling her? How could she help? She had just walked into the answer to her prayers—a God-sized impossible situation!

The rest of the story is a book in itself (in fact, Lazarus has written the book, *Shoes for the Footless*). My wife simply kept praying and got on the phone. Within forty-eight hours, the baby was under my brother's care, his parents were here in America, and newspapers were writing about the miracle.

When the family arrived in Atlanta, they changed planes and flew to South Carolina, where my brother practices. At the same time they were about to leave Atlanta, I was leaving to go to a speaking engagement. So before I boarded my plane, I checked to see what gate their flight was leaving from. It was next to mine! I walked over to the gate and told the ticket agent the story. They had already heard who was on the plane and allowed me to walk on and see them without a ticket.

Can you imagine the scene as I walked down the aisle and embraced this family? We turned the airplane into a sanctuary as I prayed over that sweet baby and her parents. The passion of God could have fueled the plane that day!

Though her odds of survival were almost zero, baby Victoria is alive today, living with her family in our city. Lazarus and Joy are faithful leaders in our church, and they have a new son, Isaac, who is as healthy as can be. Lazarus is now doing high-level research as a microbiologist, seeking a cure for AIDS. In his spare time, he helps coordinate our mission work in his native Africa.

Every time we see this family, we remember that there is an empty grave in Africa because of an empty tomb in Jerusalem. And God let us be right in the middle of it! That's real life. That's the Passion Promise.

Do you see evidence of God-sized passion in your life? Does your daily existence "measure up"? Is your life beginning to look just a little more like the life of a person of authentic passion?

If not, I encourage you to start asking the right questions. Run toward the love of God, toward passionate relationships, and toward impossible situations. You'll find that God will meet you there with more life than you can get your arms around.

chapter five

BETTER THAN A
DREAM COME TRUE

"Than all we ask or imagine..."

*S*OCIOLOGISTS TELL US of a strange trend taking place in the United States. Despite all the affluence, entertainment, and diversions available to us, more people are bored today than perhaps any time in our history.

Researchers at Yankelovich Partners conclude that America is stuck in a "boredom boom" in which "everything is predictable." *USA Today* columnist Walter Shapiro writes that "boredom has become a major societal trend."[6]

How can this possibly be? We have the whole world at our fingertips with just a few keystrokes on the computer. The technology for movies and video games is increasing exponentially. Manufacturers are producing the most captivating toys for children—and for adults, too—that the world has ever seen.

Recently I had the unexpected opportunity to go to the White House and meet President Bush. My sister was talking to my young nephew Lee about it. She said, "Isn't it amazing that your uncle was right there with the president of the United States?" Lee said, "Yeah, I'm just amazed that I got through level six of Frogger!" (That's a video game, for those of you even more out of touch with technology than I am.)

It's hard to impress kids these days with all the incredible stimuli bombarding their senses. There's something new to explore every day. I still can hardly believe that I wrote this book on a handheld computer that fits in my pocket.

With so many of these technically advanced products available to us, how on earth can we be bored? Maybe the answer is in the question. Could it be that we are bored because nothing *on earth* can fully captivate a human spirit that was made to find complete joy only in his or her Creator?

Eric Liddell, the subject of the movie *Chariots of Fire*, would not run on Sunday because of his convictions, but he won an Olympic gold medal anyway in another event for which he had not trained. At one point his sister, knowing of his call to missions, asked why he didn't go on to China. Why did he have to run?

Liddell said, "God made me for China, but He also made me fast. And when I run, I feel His pleasure." Wow! That's it, don't you think? Since we were made in His image, we will never really know pleasure until we feel *His* pleasure!

Perhaps our biggest problem is that, in this modern age, so many of our dreams *are* realized. Even the very young are seeing their dreams come true. Growing up, I used to day-dream about flying in an airplane. It seemed like an impossible fantasy—to actually fly. It was rare to hear about any of my friends flying. Finally, at seventeen, I took my first flight on a Piedmont Airlines commercial jet. I still remember the feeling of wonder as we lifted into the wild blue yonder.

Things are a little different for my children and their friends. They've been flying since they were babies and get upset if they don't get an aisle seat. So many in our affluent culture are saying "been there, done that" before they even grow up.

One of the most depressing experiences in life is to see all your dreams come true—and realize that you're still unhappy. I met former football star Deion Sanders a few years ago, and he told me that after both of his Super Bowl victories, he went to his hotel room and cried himself to sleep. Deion won two world championships and was miserable. It wasn't until he discovered passion in Jesus Christ that he found true fulfillment. It was a freedom he'd never felt while realizing his dreams on his own.

Recently I've become deeply frustrated trying to help a great professional athlete who still hasn't figured out Deion's secret. My friend made his millions, threw it all away, and then tried every other conceivable thing to make himself happy. He continues on this downward spiral because though he says he believes in Jesus, he refuses to give Him a chance to really *be* his life. I love this friend. I hurt for him and grieve for what he's missing. But I can't change him. Only Jesus can do that. And He will if my friend will only let Him.

And then there are those who are still waiting for their

first dream to come true. People with little or nothing still dream. They dream of what many of us already have. When I was in Uganda, I talked with a teenage boy whose father had died of AIDS and whose mother was near death from the same disease. Soon to be an orphan on the street, he looked at me with fire in his eyes and said, "I want to be the first in my family to *be* something!"

I believe he will. But the truth is, even if he "becomes something," even if his dreams come true, the day will arrive when he will begin to have a nagging sense that he is missing something. And he will be—unless he finds that Something better than a dream come true.

THE BIGGEST KINGDOM

Let's get personal. What about *you?* Do you *really* believe Jesus? Or do you just want Him around when you need Him?

If you really believe Jesus, then you will hear Him when He says that your own dreams will never cut it. They will leave you lifeless and drifting even if every last one of them comes true. To really believe Jesus means that you have aligned yourself with a kingdom. You aren't just looking for a heavenly errand boy to run and get you what you want. You're pledging your allegiance to a King.

Jesus said, "Seek first his kingdom and his righteousness, and all these things will be given to you as well" (Matthew 6:33). Pretty amazing words. He is the King and your life is His kingdom. Seek to serve Him in His kingdom and you will find joy in your own life. Seek to build your own kingdom and you will find nothing worth having at all.

The concept of the kingdom of God is one of the most important subjects in the Bible, but it may be one of the least understood by believers. Jesus talked about the kingdom of God more than He talked about love, grace, faith, joy, forgiveness, or even salvation. Why? Because all those things and more are found *within* the kingdom. This was the heart and soul of the message and mission of Jesus. He came "preaching the good news of the kingdom" (Matthew 4:23).

During your life you can be a citizen of one of two kingdoms. Either by choice or by default, you can be a citizen of the kingdom of this world—a kingdom ruled by a temporary king in which all your passion will be temporary as well (Ephesians 2:2).

Or you can choose the kingdom of God.

These kingdoms are not geographical in nature. In fact, both can exist in the same school, business, home, or church. In the kingdom of this world, you can dream big dreams. Some of them may even come true. The king of this world is happy to help out with that as long as they are only *your* dreams. Satan knows that those dreams can look so captivating that they hide what you are really missing. Because in the kingdom of God you pursue more than your dreams. The kingdom of God is bigger than your dreams. It *belongs* to God! It's as big as He is.

So how do you get in on this? How do you make sure you're living in the right kingdom? Whenever someone submits to Jesus as King and acknowledges that true passion is found only in His reign, the kingdom of God has come to that life! It is vitally important to choose the right kingdom.

A few years ago I met the Iraqi ambassador to the United

Nations. As I talked with him, attempting to build a relationship in which I could share the gospel, he invited me to come and visit his country. Can you imagine the scene if I had arrived at the ambassador's door during the recent war with Iraq and asked for a tour of Baghdad? He would have thought I was crazy!

And he would have been right. It was no time for a tourist trip to the kingdom of Iraq. There's no pleasure to be found during a war. And there's no passion to be found in the kingdom of this world—not authentic passion. Don't try being a tourist! Why would you?

One day soon there will be only one kingdom. Revelation 11:15 looks to that day: "The seventh angel sounded his trumpet, and there were loud voices in heaven, which said: 'The kingdom of this world has become the kingdom of our Lord and of his Christ, and he will reign for ever and ever.'" Since there will be only one kingdom soon, why not live in that kingdom now?

LIVING A LIFE ONLY GOD CAN IMAGINE

The Passion Promise says, "You are designed for a life of passion—a life only God can imagine." That's because there *is* something better than a dream come true. And that's living right in the middle of a life you never could dream of, because it's bigger than you! *More than all we ask or imagine.*

The Greek word translated *imagine* in Ephesians 3:20 can also mean "to deeply understand." Hebrews 11:3 says, "By faith we *understand* that the universe was formed at God's command, so that what is seen was not made out of what is visible."

Same word. Do you get this? We can understand at least something of the creation of the universe. We can look up at the stars and study them with telescopes. We can send spaceships to do complex tests to understand other worlds. But no telescope can peer into the magnificence of God's dream for you. No spacecraft can travel there. Only God can take you there. He loves you deeply and has plans for your life so wonderful, so much bigger than you, that you can't even imagine or understand them. But you can live them.

Think about it this way. Stop and dream for a moment. What is the greatest thing you can imagine God doing in your life in the next year? In your family? In your church? God says that whatever you have imagined, you have not scratched the surface of the reality of what He wants to do.

You've just read it, but do you believe it? Do you see that God really loves you this much?

If this is true and you begin to live like it is, your life will never be the same. The central theme of this book will begin to become reality in your life—you will never have another boring day.

You are ready to begin living out the Passion Promise. But how does it work in the real world?

MORE THAN YOU CAN IMAGINE— EVERY DAY

Realize first that this promise is not just for those once-in-a-lifetime moments you tell everyone about or, if you're like me, write about in a book. This promise for everyday life experiences.

Notice that I didn't say *ordinary* life experiences. Take the word *ordinary* out of your spiritual vocabulary. If God truly is as intimately involved in your life as He claims to be, then there is absolutely nothing ordinary about this day or any other day. But what about the everyday stuff? How does the Passion Promise work when nothing unusual seems to be happening? When the day just seems like the same old routine?

Well, if we want Him to, if we will open our eyes and look, God always does one of two things with what seems ordinary. He either makes it extraordinary or makes it silently significant—and either one can change your life!

It's All Significant

You have to decide whether you really believe that what you are doing right now, or in the next five minutes, *matters*. And you have to look for why it matters. Are you willing to trust that even if your day seemed completely insignificant, God has used you in significant ways because you asked Him to? Even if you don't see the results of His work right now?

For instance, does taking a shower in the morning somehow matter (beyond not smelling bad)? These days there are two certain people that I want to pray for with unusual intensity, so I pray for them every morning in the shower. When I feel the water hit my skin, I know that I am standing in the flow of the presence of God. My shower has become significant!

If you miss an airline flight, is that somehow spiritually significant? Of course it is. God is at work. Get ready. Look around.

I wish I could say that I always practice what I preach. I remember once being so frustrated because I had missed my flight. While I was fuming as I boarded the next flight, a man introduced himself to me. He had heard me preach before but was struggling with his long-held agnosticism. That conversation began a long relationship, and today he is a teacher in our church.

Will an agnostic come to know Christ every time you miss a flight? Probably not, but God is always up to something. There's something to learn or someone to touch or somewhere God wants you to be—or not be. That's how He works. *There is no ordinary.*

When you are sleeping, God is preparing you for tomorrow. When you are playing, He is rejoicing over you. When you are doing the laundry, He is shaping you. When you are bored with your job, He is pointing you to the real reason you're there.

If you're a student, I want you to realize that study hall matters. In fact, where you *sit* in study hall matters. I know.

On August 31, 2003, I stood on the stage at a Christian concert to share the good news of Jesus with thousands gathered there. The concert was held on the football field of Hendersonville High School in western North Carolina—*my* old high school and the field where I'd played football. I had come home.

It was an emotional night for me. I had the chance to talk with old friends, walk on the field where I had played, and share my passion for Jesus and His plan for our lives.

As I spoke to the crowd that night, I was able to look across the field and see the window of the classroom where the course of my life changed. My thoughts drifted back to 1975. It was an "ordinary" school day. I was in study hall. I don't remember much about it except that a girl named Dottie was sitting in front of me. She turned around and invited me to come to church that night and hear her youth choir sing. She seemed a little nervous. I didn't have a clue that she was trying to witness to me.

I went to church most Sundays back then, but had never really heard the gospel. I'd certainly never heard of the Jesus Movement. I had no idea that God's Spirit was sweeping through students across America. I just knew that a pretty blonde had invited me somewhere, and that was enough reason to go!

That night I went to an evangelical church for the first time in my life. I heard young people sing with passion. I heard a man speak with power. And I met Jesus! I've never recovered.

When you're a teenager, sometimes you take for granted the things people do for you. After I graduated and went on to college in Texas, it bothered me that I had never said thank you to Dottie. The years went by and I never saw her again.

In 1998, it was time for our twenty-year high school reunion, where we would get to see the toll time had taken on us all. But spiritually, time had been very good to me. The decision to follow Jesus had affected every part of my life. I had a life with purpose and passion, and there was someone I needed to thank. I recognized Dottie from across the room and walked over to her. We went through all the normal updates of our lives, and then I said, "Dottie, I owe you an apology for never saying thank you for helping me find the greatest gift in my life."

Dottie had no idea what I was talking about. I reminded her of her invitation to me in study hall so many years ago. "Yes, I do remember that!" she said.

"Well, it changed my life, Dottie. It's twenty years late, but thank you—with all my heart."

Tears welled up in Dottie's eyes as she told me of the recent death of her husband. She said, "You know, I've sometimes wondered if my life was making any difference."

"Dottie," I said, "for the rest of your life, if you are ever tempted to wonder if your life counts, please know this: Every good thing in my life—my wife, my children, my church, my joy, my passion, and anyone that I may have ever touched—I owe all of that to you!"

Your life counts. All of it. The next moment of it. It is all significant. That's the Passion Promise.

Changing Ordinary into Extraordinary

Then there are those times when God makes the "ordinary" extraordinary. Often He will do this when you least expect it. That's why life should never be boring. The next moment might just change your life forever. It's also why we need to know Him intimately and walk with Him closely—so we don't miss that life-changing moment that's just around the corner.

It was January 22, 1995. I was the pastor of Coggin Avenue Baptist Church in Brownwood, Texas. Things had not been going well. In fact, I wondered whether I was even in the right place. I was preaching about the Ten Commandments at the 8 A.M. service. Excitement was in the air. Well, not really. I was just glad that most of the congregation seemed to be awake.

But at the end of the service everything changed. A student named Chris from Howard Payne University came forward and asked me if he could say a word. That was strange. I checked the bulletin—Chris wasn't listed.

I look back on that day and wonder what would have happened if I had told Chris to talk to me later. After all, it was time for Sunday school. I think I know—if I had put Chris off, God would have found another place where He could do what He wanted to do that day. I miss so much of what God's up to, but I'm sure glad I didn't miss it that day.

As Chris poured out his heart about the state of our church and his school and shared his desperate burden that the time for revival had come, God began to break the hearts of His people. Suddenly people there were flooding the aisles! People began to weep, to come to Christ, to publicly ask forgiveness for sin, to reconcile with each other. Most never made it to Sunday school that day. This amazing revival at our church went on through the Sunday school hour, through the late service, and into the early afternoon. We came back that night and it kept on going. We were there for hours! God did in one day what I had not been able to do in three years.

Powerful movements of God began on that same day at other churches in Brownwood, where pastors had been praying together for revival. Then a similar movement broke out on the campus of Howard Payne University as ministry leader Henry Blackaby spoke and led the students in revival. Students in Texas public schools began to form prayer and fasting clubs and lead their friends to Christ at lunch.

It spread further. Week after week people came from all over to join us as God moved. Revival broke out on the campus of Southwestern Seminary, Wheaton College, and then at dozens of schools across America. We could hardly believe what was happening. Our office became like a travel agency as staff, students, and regular folks from the pews went out to tell the story. Our police chief spoke at churches, and our fire chief became a missionary. The *Associated Press* came and covered the story. Newspapers and magazines wrote about it. Even Phil Donahue did a show about it. Our church exploded in growth, hundreds of people were saved, wonderful racial reconciliation came to many in our city, and for two years students across the nation embraced God's Spirit in a new and amazing way.

On the day I wrote this chapter, I was preaching in Wilmington, North Carolina. One of the students who was at Howard Payne during those days saw my name on the church sign and came to hear me. Marti is married now, with a new baby, and is faithfully serving with her husband in a church staff position. Reflecting on the revival, Marti said, "There is only one negative about it for me. Now I am never satisfied with anything less than what we experienced. I want to see God do things that only He can do!"

To this day, I meet people almost everywhere I go who tell me they will never be the same because of how they encountered God in those years. I am one of those people, too. Who has ever heard of Brownwood, Texas? God has! He is the God of passion who just may step into the next moment of your life and change the ordinary into the extraordinary.

Are you ready?

LEAVING BOREDOM BEHIND

Whatever God is doing in your life, the significant or the extraordinary, your responsibility for living daily in the life only God can imagine is the same. Here are five steps toward doing just that.

1. Seek Him every day

God wants a personal relationship with you. But like any other relationship, you'll never know Him on an intimate level—or begin to see the life He has imagined for you—unless you spend regular time with Him. We're blessed to have a merciful God, one who is always ready to forgive our long absences and again welcome us into His presence. But He won't force Himself on us—we must *choose* to be in His presence.

As you seek Him, don't forget to praise Him for His passion and the life He has imagined for you. Your words of adoration will bring joy to heaven.

2. Look for Him to work

Expect God to be at work in your life. Look especially for the unusual things that spark your sense that God is up to something. Remember, Jesus told the disciples, "Anyone who has faith in me will do what I have been doing. He will do *even greater things* than these" (John 14:12). When our faith is strong, we can expect to influence even more people and nations than Jesus Himself did while on earth! That's a life only God can imagine.

But don't miss God's handiwork by overlooking what at

first seems absolutely insignificant. Just read the Bible. God loves to show up to shepherds, stutterers, and teenagers. And He often does His greatest work when we least expect it.

I think God enjoys working this way. He loves to surprise us—just as a father takes joy in surprising his children. Many times He will surprise you when you are simply *with* Him. There's no earth-shattering event going on. You're just quietly spending time with Him.

It's important to understand that a life without boredom—a life only God can imagine—is not a life of perpetual activity. That will just wear you out and eventually leave you tired and bored anyway. Take the time to *listen* to and *look* for Him. He has far more adventure for you than you can ever run after. Be sure to have regular times when you are simply quiet before Him. If you don't, you will likely run right past the greatest moments of your life. Slow down and keep your spiritual eyes open. He's at work!

3. Accept God's call to act where He is working

If God put you where He is active, then you are the one He wants to use there. That's exciting, maybe even scary—but definitely not boring! Realize, though, that God's specific call on you, the ways He wants to use you, may not seem full of passion at first. His call may look like the opposite of passion.

Just a few months ago, I saw one of the greatest pictures of the Passion Promise lived out that I've ever seen. I went to visit a family that our church has ministered to for years, the Murphys. I felt bad that I had never met them personally. Because our church is so large, no one expects me to visit in every home, but this family was unique.

I didn't go to their house expecting to see passion personified. Actually, I thought I was going in order to encourage some people who I was sure must have an almost unbearable existence. You see, the Murphys have *twenty-eight children*! As they will tell you, four are now with the Lord, and three are on their own, but twenty-one are in the house right now. Most of their children are adopted and have severe mental handicaps. They live in a modest home in the south Atlanta area and are both full-time parents and caregivers. John, the father, trained as a nurse to be able to care for his family's medical needs. Jeanette is as loving a mom as you will ever find.

I really expected to walk into a chaotic atmosphere, but when I arrived I was absolutely stunned. Their children were happy and fulfilled. Everyone had responsibilities and everyone gave and received lots of love. There were even two new babies among the throng!

The whole situation was beyond my comprehension. John and Jeanette are models of Christian parenting. When I asked how in the world their home was such a place of peace, responsibility, and love, John just smiled and said, "Biblical parenting really works when you try it."

Both John and Jeanette had lived lives totally apart from God. They were a part of the hippie culture, partaking in the alcohol and drugs that went with it. But when they met Jesus, they found real passion—and a call to adopt and love children that others didn't want. Throughout our conversation, I kept thinking, *These people actually look happy!* Finally I just asked, "Are you happy with your life?"

"Are you kidding?" Jeanette said. "Who could have a better life? We have Christ and these wonderful children to love. We have more joy than we know what to do with."

This flies in the face of everything the world says about what will give you real passion, doesn't it? But a person of authentic passion is not running after the stuff the world offers. Like the Murphys, he *rejects imitations* and *focuses on the Creator.* A person of authentic passion, like the Murphys, *always expects joyful passion,* sometimes in the strangest places. And a person of authentic passion, like the Murphys, *shares it with others*—including "the least of these" (Matthew 25:40), the neglected or forgotten children.

On Easter Sunday last year, our congregation sang the song "He's Alive!" at all three services. The Murphy children came up during the chorus and sang it with our soloist. I probably don't have to tell you that the atmosphere in that place was electric. It was the resurrection power of Jesus lived out before us.

My point is not that you need to adopt as many children as you can. My point is that you must answer God's call to act where He is working with *you.* And He is working. Don't miss it!

4. Tell others what happens

Most believers never see God work this way. They're not even looking for Him. They might not even be at church. Help them see how God really works. David said in Psalm 71:17, "Since my youth, O God, you have taught me, and to this day I declare your marvelous deeds." Start right now, and for the rest of your life tell people what God is up to.

If all of God's people would begin talking about what He

is doing as much as they gossip about the latest rumor or complain about the problems in their churches, we would all soon be overwhelmed with the presence and power of God. Spread the word of His Passion Promise until no one can miss it!

5. Trust God completely

It's easy to put your faith in God when everything you set out to do falls quickly into place, but it's a different matter when you don't immediately see the results you hoped for. Realize that while God is at work in the "now," He is also using now to paint the picture that will exist in a hundred years. Are you ready to trust Him completely? Are you willing to believe that your life will matter long after you're gone—if you choose the life only God can imagine?

Occasionally I take our staff on a team-building field trip. Recently I told them to bundle up and get on the bus. No one knew where we were going. We drove to a remote, ancient cemetery I had found in the woods while hunting.

When we got off the bus at the graveyard, they looked at me like I was crazy. I told them to walk around for about a half hour and then tell me what they had learned about life and leadership. (Hmm…graveyard leadership lessons. Sounds like another book to me!)

One member of the team found a very old tombstone from the early nineteenth century. It had been carved by a husband who obviously loved his wife very much. On it was the passage that described her life: "Whatever your hand finds to do, do it with all your might" (Ecclesiastes 9:10).

We stood there talking about the life this woman must

have lived. She died young, but had made such a great impact on her husband that he wanted all the world to know that his wife lived passionately in all she did, with all her might, for her family and her God. Her husband wanted us to know that—and now we did. And it changed us.

We took a picture of that tombstone back with us, showed it to thousands of people on the big screen at church, and told what we knew of the story. In heaven, I bet this woman danced with passion. For an obscure woman buried in an obscure place was now being talked about in another age. Her life still mattered!

I'll bet that she dances still as you read this. Dance with her! You have a life that's better than a dream come true. So get ready to get up tomorrow morning and leave boredom behind. It will be God's day to work passionately in and through your life. That's how you live day by day the life that only God can imagine.

chapter six

A BOXER OR A SOLDIER?

"According to his power that is at work within us..."

B Y NOW YOU MIGHT be tempted to just memorize the Passion Promise, say it four times a day facing north, south, east, and west, and expect to happily go on your way to a magical life, where good things meet you at every turn.

Though I sometimes hear messages like that from television preachers, I never read them in the Bible. God's promise to you is life without boring days, not life without bad days. The Passion Promise is not just about the wonderful ways God is at work in your life; it is also about the bloody and crucial battle you are in.

According to his power...

Everything we accomplish in life is utterly dependent on

God's power. The Greek word for power is *dunamis,* from which we draw our word *dynamite.* It's an explosive word! If there is no opposition, no one who fights against you, then you do not need power. But if you find yourself in the middle of the battlefield, wounded and wondering if you can go on one more minute, then God's power is everything you need.

Take away the explosive power of God in a person's life and the Passion Promise is no more than the latest pop psychology. Only the power of God arms you to run through the most terrifying, most dangerous, most pain-filled battlefields of your life and not only win, but win with joy!

Power is one of the most important words in the Bible, and it's one of the most important words for your journey. It is used to describe Jesus' power to heal, His power over demons, His power to save. The apostle Peter says, "His divine *power* has given us everything we need for life and godliness" (2 Peter 1:3).

Wow—everything we need! This is important stuff. His power does *not* give us everything we need for a comfortable life. But it is everything we need for the war.

Paul says, "But join with me in suffering for the gospel, by the *power* of God" (2 Timothy 1:8). Are you willing to suffer for the gospel? Or are you just reading this book to find out how you can be more successful?

The Passion Promise is a call to give up our own pursuits, abandoning everything for Jesus and His good news for the world. The wonderful irony is that when we do risk everything for Jesus, we discover the incredible joy of resting in His passion.

But no one who chooses this road escapes the battlefield.

Training for Battle

Are you still with me? Good. Then let's train for the battle.

The words we just read from Paul give us two wonderful training tips. First, God's power is *enough* for you when you suffer. Paul says he suffers "by the power of God." On the surface those are strange words.

One of the great wonders I've encountered in more than twenty years as a pastor is how God's people face deep grief with amazing peace. I have seen people lose their loved ones in almost every conceivable way, and though their pain is almost unbearable, they win their battle against suffering. I have often been afraid of how I would handle the losses I have seen others suffer. As I speak to many such people about this, they almost always say the same thing: "We would never have believed that we could come through this. The power of God alone sustained us."

I'll always remember the first time I really saw God's power at work in the midst of unbearable pain. I was a new believer—just a kid trying to understand this new relationship with God that was rocking every part of my world. Our youth group went on a swimming outing at Lake Lure in the mountains of North Carolina, but I couldn't go because I'd just had oral surgery.

Later, my friend David came to the house to tell me what had happened. I knew something was wrong as soon as I saw his face. Cowboy was gone. His real name was Keith Robinson, but we all called him Cowboy because he was the only guy we knew who wore a cowboy hat and boots. Cowboy jumped off a boat dock into the water that day and never came back up.

For the first time in my life, death had come calling for someone I knew, someone I cared about. It came suddenly and left me frightened and confused. Didn't God take care of those who loved Him? Was the God I had just recently come to know really who I thought He was? Could I trust Him?

At the funeral our youth choir sang Cowboy's favorite song. He'd always stood right by me when we sang it: "Someday a bright new wave will break upon the shore, and there'll be no sickness, no more sorrow, no more war. And little children never will go hungry anymore. And they'll be a bright new morning over there. There'll be a bright new world for us to share."

Even as I type these words I am singing it. Remembering it.

When the service was over, we all walked past the casket. Death was suddenly so ugly and real to me. Just beyond the casket were Cowboy's parents. Everyone was saying something to them. I was terrified. I had nothing to say. No comfort to offer. I wanted to run, but instead I just walked up to them and cried.

Then something happened that I have seen many times since. But that day, that first time, it was the decisive, winning blow in the battle for this young man's faith. *They* comforted *me!* They both threw their arms around me and said, "Don't worry, John. It's all right. Cowboy is with Jesus right now. This very minute."

Cowboy's mom and dad held on to me. In their arms I found something—a faith that was rock-solid while the world was reeling. This Jesus stuff was real! It worked on the battlefield and at the cemetery just as surely as it worked at church.

I found myself wanting to know more about the richness and wonder of this power. I still do.

Always remember: Your King does not send you to the battlefield without all you need. His power is enough for you—even when you suffer.

Paul's second training tip is found in his words "Join with me." Paul knew how crucial it is to fight together. Most believers never really get this. If they are in the battle at all, they fight like boxers rather than soldiers.

Think about it. Boxers fight alone, in the arena they choose, using their own strength, under their own authority, and for themselves. A soldier fights too, but his approach is completely different. He fights *together* with an army. He fights in the arena where his commander sends him. He fights under the authority of another. He does not fight in his own strength alone—he uses the weapons and tools he is given. He is often helped in the battle by air support and other parts of the army he has nothing to do with.

When the victory is won, the soldier is not celebrated as the victor. He has won for his king and for the kingdom. You see, a boxer is playing a game, while a soldier is engaged in a life-and-death war. You are a soldier, not a boxer! So how does the Passion Promise equip you to fight this war? Let's look at your battle plan.

FIGHTING ONLY GOD'S BATTLES

As a soldier you do not have the right to decide which battles you will fight. In fact, a soldier who runs to a battle without being commanded to is at best a detriment to the army and at worst a traitor. Remember—it is *His power* that is in us, so it must be His decision when and where we fight.

I cannot stress how important this is. I have the opportunity to preach across America, and I am constantly struck by how many people in our churches are fighting the wrong battles. We are like those U.S. Army "jelly searchers." While people all around us are bleeding and dying in real battles, we find ourselves covered with grape jelly, crawling around searching for more. The time believers waste and the devastation we cause by fighting our own battles is, I am convinced, one of the great tragedies of our day.

How do we know which battles are God's? Ask yourself these questions before charging off to war.

Do I have a clear word from the Commander?

It really doesn't matter how strongly you feel about a battle or how certain you are of the justice of the cause. The only question is: Has God ordered you to the front lines? Make sure you have heard from Him through His Word and through much intimate time with Him.

When we spend time with God, praying and listening, He *does* speak to us by the power "at work within us." We hear His voice through the Spirit of truth, the Holy Spirit. Jesus said, "I will ask the Father, and he will give you another Counselor to be with you forever—the Spirit of truth…. You know him, for he lives with you and will be *in you*" (John 14:16–17).

This Counselor is God's gift to us, the Spirit dwelling *within* us and linking us to God's power. It is God's Spirit that brings a person into your life at just the right moment, with counsel that makes your course clear. It is God's Spirit that brings about circumstances that are too "coincidental" to be coincidence, which point like a road sign in the direction you should go. The Commander will not send you to fight without His clear orders. When we hear God telling us through the voice of the Spirit that a conflict is at hand, we'd better be ready to fight!

A good way to judge whether you are correctly interpreting the Spirit's voice is to find out if the best members of the army are hearing the same command. If you rush onto the battlefield with no officers accompanying you, it may mean you've misinterpreted your instruction from the Commander.

When I am considering entering the fray, I always take counsel from the most seasoned, mature spiritual warriors I know. Without exception, whenever I have charged into battle against their counsel, I have made a serious mistake.

Is this battle against the right enemy?

Do not miss this: The battles God calls us to fight are never against people! In Ephesians, the same book of the Bible that contains the foundation of the Passion Promise, God makes this clear: "For our struggle is not against flesh and blood, but against the rulers, against the authorities, against the powers of this dark world and against the spiritual forces of evil in the heavenly realms" (6:12). Now that's a war!

People who don't know Christ are not our enemy. They are our *mission*. We should never be surprised when unbelievers oppose us or treat us unfairly. We are to love them, not fight them. We *do* need to resist what unbelievers stand for. Anything less would mean abdicating our call to be salt and light. But though we may oppose some people's choices or lifestyles, we must never oppose *them*. Instead, we let them see the mysterious mixture of power and love within us—an action they'll never see anywhere else.

Imagine what might happen if those who most strongly opposed abortion were also the leaders in ministry to single moms. Or if those who took the strongest stands against the homosexual agenda also did the most to minister to those impacted by AIDS. That's the Jesus way to make a difference, and the right way to fight God's battles.

God's people aren't our enemy either, though by the division in our churches today that seems a truth we have trouble remembering. When we have a problem with a believer, we are to love, forgive, and humbly seek healing. If that doesn't work, we still are not called to war but to respond like Jesus, even if we are hurt. Paul could not believe that the Corinthians would fight each other, even to the point of going to court against fellow church members. He said, "The very fact that you have lawsuits among you means you have been completely defeated already. Why not rather be wronged? Why not rather be cheated?" (1 Corinthians 6:7).

Unbelievably, such conflicts have become a major issue of concern for churches today. Every church has to be insured and aware of a multitude of liability issues. I might be able to understand churches being sued by unbelievers, but Christians suing the church and each other? Refusing to reconcile disagreements within the church and even taking money from God's own people in secular lawsuits? How can this happen? And yet it *is* happening, all across the country.

Some believers live as if they can disregard God's instruction to them because they are sure they are right or because that's what everyone does these days. But we are to be *different*! The precise meaning of the Greek translation for *church* is "called out." As members of God's church, we are called out from the way a world without Christ lives and called into His passion and love.

You are never in the right battle if you're fighting your brother or sister. If that's where you are, God says you are already defeated. Our enemy is a spiritual one. Our enemy is the author of hatred, division, and evil. If God is calling you to battle, He is calling you to fight *that* enemy—and only that one.

Are you trying to fix what only God can fix?

We humans seem to have an innate desire to straighten things out, as if we think God can't get along without us. We often fight on the wrong battlefield because we see a problem and are just sure we're the ones to correct it. When we step in, we end up in a mess. Because of our foolish pride, we fail to understand the truth about the problem we're trying to fix, or we try to fix the wrong problem altogether.

I've learned one thing over the years: God is the "fixer," not me! Everyone who knows me well understands that I am a disaster waiting to happen when it comes to fixing, repairing, or building anything. About half the time I change a lightbulb, I either shock myself or blow out the power. Don't ask me how it happens. It's just my gift.

So I have learned to ask for help. When I do, people in my church feel sorry for me and willingly come over to protect me and help me with things that normally cause me bodily harm.

I know my weaknesses. I am not a fixer and should not try to fix what I am not equipped to handle. Neither should you. If the fight before you is just an effort to fix something, leave it to God and stay off that battlefield.

Are you fighting too many battles at once?

Many people seem to thrive on controversy and warfare, drawing their sense of purpose from the next battle to be fought. They run from battle to battle, frequently lashing out in multiple directions. Not only are they ineffective soldiers, they often end up hurting those they think they're helping. This is a hard area for me to keep in line.

Recently, I felt the pull to enter a battle among some of our church members that had all the marks of being a distraction. The people involved had launched a "fix-it" campaign that I believed included gossip and half-truths—some of them about me.

I hadn't heard a call from the Commander. I knew exactly what God had called me to do, and it was not this battle. Still, I felt drawn to it. The pull came from my own pride. I held information that would set things straight. Surely I ought to put aside for just a while what the Commander had told me to do in order to clear up this mess. Right?

Wrong. One of the hardest battlefield lessons to learn is how to reject the temptation to defend yourself and let God be your defender instead. Otherwise—and this is so important—*the battle becomes about you!*

It's not supposed to be about you. Or me. If we sink to that lower-level battlefield, we're in danger of spending the rest of our lives in bitter self-centeredness. Paul says, "See to it that no one misses the grace of God and that no bitter root grows up to cause trouble and defile many" (Hebrews 12:15). Bitterness will only cause trouble for you and hurt those around you.

"But what," you may ask, "if I am misunderstood or treated unfairly? What if people lie about me or even hate me without just cause?" Then praise God—you have joined the experience of Jesus!

That doesn't make it easy, though, does it?

Even though I knew I was following Jesus, one of the hardest things was to just be quiet in that battle within our church. Not only did God take us through that battle, He used it to prepare our church for greater things. But it is never pleasant in the midst of the fight.

God used a powerful section of our war manual, His Word, to encourage me. I was studying the life of David and was amazed by how he dealt with the tragedy of his own son Absalom's rebellion against him. As David was fleeing his own city, a man named Shimei began to curse him and throw stones and mud at him. David's friend wanted to kill him. But David knew that there was a much more important battle to fight. *He would not turn aside to fight a bully and leave the real war behind.*

David said, "It may be that the LORD will see my distress and repay me with good for the cursing I am receiving today" (2 Samuel 16:12).

Incredible! David was willing to put absolute trust in the Lord to be his vindicator so he could fight the right battle. Are you willing to trust God like that even when the rocks and dirt are flying at you? The sense of security that comes from releasing your right to defend yourself and instead leaving it up to God is astounding.

Later, David was pressed to execute Shimei. He was wise enough never to trust the man again, but also wise enough to let God be his defender. He said, "Do I not know that today I am king over Israel?" (2 Samuel 19:22).

Now that's a man with his head on straight, who fights the right battles! David didn't need vengeance to boost his ego. He knew exactly who he was and who he served, and he refused to be turned aside by misplaced fights. I want to be like that! I often fail at it, but I'm determined to invest my life on the right battlefield.

Will this battle matter forever?

This question really helps me. Life is short. We just don't have time to fight battles that won't matter or be remembered in fifty years—or even in fifty days. I want to invest my life in what is eternally significant. This rules out most of the conflicts that tempt me to take up my sword.

So...you have carefully listened to God's call to battle; you've answered each of these important questions; and you now know that you are on the right battlefield. What's the next step in the battle plan?

KNOW *HOW* TO FIGHT

Nothing is more important to a soldier than learning *how* to fight. A soldier won't accomplish anything if he makes it to the right battlefield but doesn't know how to use his weapons. So how, specifically, do we use the power God gives us? How do we fight?

Use Your Superior Power

"The prayer of a righteous man is powerful and effective" (James 5:16). That's pretty straightforward. If you run past prayer, you run past power!

I recently called our church to forty days of prayer and fasting. We prayed for every member of our church. We prayed for a new missions work we are beginning. We prayed for God's passion and power in our church. I told them what I know is true for me, for them, for us all—no prayer, no passion, no power. Great prayer, great passion, great power! That's God's way.

Do you struggle in this area? I think nearly the whole body of Christ does. We shouldn't be surprised. If God's passion and power begin with prayer, it makes sense that this would be our enemy's front line of attack against us. One of the most common things I hear, even from mature believers, is that they struggle to spend much significant time with God. I can relate!

Maybe that surprises you. Don't all pastors spend hours on their knees? Actually, my suspicion is that pastors aren't much different from other believers in the time they spend with God. I know that at times in my ministry, I have almost totally neglected my devotional time. I'm ashamed of that. What's really scary is that I know how to do ministry without prayer. I can still preach and do "church stuff" without prayer. But I also know that when the power of God is hindered in my life, it will show sooner or later. And even when others don't notice my distance from my Father, I do. And worst of all, He does! These days I am after Him. I don't want any more powerless periods in my ministry.

But what do we do about these dry times? It helps me to remember that God is not a legalist. I don't have to spend my time with Him in the same ways in every season of my life. A devotional life is a discipline, but more than that, it is a relationship.

I have found that varying how I relate to God helps keep me from burning out or settling into a rut. I stay fresh with Him. So, though I have a prayer corner where I regularly hit my knees, sometimes I will spend far more prayer time jogging than kneeling. I love breathing in His love and breathing out His praises while I run. Or I'll go sit in the woods with my bow and listen for God more than for deer. God just wants to meet with you. Find a place, a time, and a way to do it for this period of your life. Just don't miss Him.

If you are fighting the right battles, you will be fighting a formidable enemy every time. Don't charge a tank with the pellet gun of your own resources. Hit your knees or whatever position helps you be in touch with Him and take on the enemy from that position of superior strength.

Speak When Others Won't

Have you ever sat silently in the presence of clear injustice because it just wasn't comfortable to speak up? It doesn't feel good later, does it? It shouldn't! God's people should raise their voices against the forces of evil.

We live in an era in which few believe in truth at all. According to our postmodern culture, evil is a myth that doesn't even exist. So let me ask you—if God's people, some of the only people who still believe in truth, won't speak out, who will?

Jesus spoke loudly and clearly against evil. He was patient and full of grace and love, but when the battle lines were drawn, Jesus made it clear where He stood. He said to some religious leaders of His day, "You snakes! You brood of vipers! How will you escape being condemned to hell?" (Matthew 23:33).

Whoa! Not much room for doubt about what Jesus thought. There are those times for all who want to follow Jesus when we too must speak—loudly, clearly, and with no compromise:

- "I'm very sorry that this pregnancy will cause you such inconvenience, but if you abort this baby you are murdering your child."
- "If you want to leave our church because God is bringing white and black people together here, we will help you pack. If you want to stay and learn to replace your racism with love, we'll help you do that, too."
- "We will not excuse your desire to leave your family for any reason whatsoever. We will confront you and your lover at every opportunity to seek to stop you from destroying the most precious gift you have."
- "Your gossip and slander is as serious to God as any sexual sin, and you will not be allowed to lead in any way in this church until you repent."

These are all statements members of our church staff have had to make. None of these statements are pleasant to hear, but they are right and true. We fight in God's strength by speaking His truth in love.

Stand Boldly in Evil's Way

Sometimes it is not enough to speak. We must act! There is a time to follow Jesus to the temple and kick out the thieves. But we better be sure the issue is crystal clear and not just an excuse for perpetuating our own anger or bitterness.

This kind of fight can even be physical, such as involvement in a just war or the protection of the innocent from evil. If, for instance, you come into my house to hurt my wife or children, I will do everything I can to stop you, even kill you if necessary. Does that sound harsh? Too bad! God has called me to protect my family, and if violence is the only way to accomplish that, I will do it without hesitation—and passionately.

An example of our more common battles is the recent court fight over saying the pledge of allegiance in our schools. The Ninth Circuit Court in California ruled that the pledge cannot be teacher-led or school-sanctioned because it contains the words *under God.* At this writing, the ruling has been stayed, but the possibility remains that the pledge could be outlawed.

I recently told our church that if this becomes law in the state of Georgia, I will urge every administrator, teacher, and student to disobey that law. I told them that I would stand with them in their schools as they say the pledge together and that, if necessary, I'd go with them to jail.

This is not Christians' usual course of action. Paul said, "Everyone must submit himself to the governing authorities" (Romans 13:1). But that changes if laws and leaders are immoral or cause us to compromise our faith (see Acts 4:19; 5:29). There *are* times when we must fight. Just be clear about which battles to fight and how to fight them, and you will never fight alone.

KNOW YOUR FELLOW SOLDIERS

According to His power that is at work within us...

Christ's power for the battle is not for you alone. You are not a boxer, but a soldier, which means you're part of a team. You need to deepen your relationships with your passion partners and fight together. Pray together about the battles you face. Guard your hearts, evaluate your strategy together by the Word of God, and don't be drawn away from "we" to "I."

Then carefully watch what God is doing around you, as we discussed in chapter 5. He will often lead you to people who need you to fight alongside them. God may know that alone they will fail, but that together you can succeed. Never assume that a new relationship God leads you into is ordinary. God is always at work, especially in relationships.

Last year, my daughter Amy and I hired a personal trainer to help us both get into better shape and to help Amy, who is a terrific volleyball player, improve her vertical jump. At least it appeared that's why we hired him. Actually, God knew that there was far more to it than that.

Dave is a great trainer and a great guy. He and I really hit it off. We often talked about spiritual things. Dave knows the Lord but had been struggling in some areas. The more we talked, the more I sensed that I was to fight a spiritual battle for him. I began to pray specifically for Dave.

So I was shocked not long after to hear that Dave had bone cancer in his leg. Suddenly this strong, athletic man needed a different kind of warrior to fight with him. I called and said, "Dave, you have trained me well. Now it's my turn to be your spiritual trainer. Training begins now!"

Dave's leg had to be amputated, but he is beating this cancer. And as we are fighting this battle together, Dave's faith and strength are growing and strengthening *me*. I watched his physical strength diminish while his spiritual strength was "pumped up."

Recently Dave shared his story with our church. It made a tremendous impact on many people. He is now in a group of men I meet with each week and has become a dear friend. I love to watch him train people at the gym. He looks like his old self again. No one really notices his slight limp, and he's in incredible shape. But he's not the same!

When Dave teaches people how to get their physical bodies in shape, I now hear him sharing his passion for the One who can transform their spiritual being, too. He's making a difference. You could ask Tina about that. She's a quadriplegic mom who has a real chance to walk again because of the encouragement and gutsy coaching of a trainer who found passion through his own suffering.

It's a privilege to be in the right battle with the right warriors beside you.

KEEP TRAINING WITH HIM

We will never be finished preparing for the battles we face. And God's power for those battles will never be depleted. We simply must resist the temptation to ever think we are ready to fight on our own. We'll get creamed if we do!

There is so much to learn about living out the Passion Promise in the heat of battle. Many people, for instance, believe they have lost their passion because they go through a time of discouragement or depression. But that's just part of the cycles of life that everyone experiences. Real passion, as we have seen, weathers those times and grows stronger.

Some of my favorite people in the Bible are the sons of Korah. Maybe you've never heard of them. Read a few of the words they wrote, such as Psalm 42 or 46. You'll be glad you did. They are a fascinating bunch.

The sons of Korah were temple singers. Their calling in life was to worship in the temple and to lead others to do the same. But when they wrote the words we now read in the Bible, they had been exiled to a strange land, far from the temple. They could not do what they were born to do. Dark depression hung over them like a shadow.

Can you relate? We've all been there, haven't we? But the sons of Korah refused to stay in depression. They wrote down what they felt. They fought back against their discouragement and regained their passion. God was at work in and through them in ways they never could have dreamed. That's how the Passion Promise works! Now all of us have the record of their struggle and their victory to encourage us when we need it the most. Just when the sons of Korah seemed to sink into despair, they grasped faith and passion again: "Put your hope in God, for I will yet praise him, my Savior and my God" (Psalm 42:11).

Do you see how sometimes the most important moments of our lives, when God is building a legacy for us, are our most painful moments? Without exile for the sons of Korah, we would not have had these words! When Billy Graham needed a word for America as he spoke at the National Cathedral after September 11, where did he look? To the sons of Korah:

> God is our refuge and strength, an ever-present help in trouble. Therefore we will not fear, though the earth give way and the mountains fall into the heart of the sea....
>
> "Be still, and know that I am God; I will be exalted among the nations, I will be exalted in the earth." The LORD Almighty is with us; the God of Jacob is our fortress." (Psalm 46:1–2, 10–11)

Do you feel their faith? Do you see their passion flowing even in the midst of their depression? That's their battle training kicking in!

The good news of the Passion Promise is that His power is *at work* in us. The Greek word for "at work" means "to continually energize." If we will keep fresh in our time with Him, stay in awe of what He has to say to us, and let Him continually train us, there will always be enough energy for the battle. Paul uses the same word in Ephesians 3:7, where he says that it is God's energizing work that allows him to do what God calls him to do. And in 4:16 he says that we do not train or fight alone, but each part of the body is "energized" to fight together as one.

Everything we have learned so far about the Passion Promise is *according to His power that is at work within us*. And that energizing power really is enough!

Expect to Win

Followers of Jesus should be the most optimistic people in the world. After all, we follow the One who has already defeated death and hell. I don't think anything else is going to be much of a problem for Him! Don't be afraid to get in the right fights. You are going to win.

I love to watch my daughter play volleyball. Amy is a dominating server. But a while back, opposing teams began calling for time whenever she would get on a roll. Then Amy would hit the next serve out. They were "icing" her.

Amy and I had a talk. I pointed out that her opponents were paying her the ultimate compliment, that every time they called a time-out, she ought to be excited. It meant she was whipping them! "Amy, when the pressure is on, you want that ball! That's your privilege, to be in the heart of the game."

Amy began to win the mind game. Recently, after a time-out, I yelled to her, "Remember, you want that ball!" She smiled at me and calmly served an ace.

The enemy will try to "ice" you, too, in a hundred different ways. But when the pressure is on, not in a game but on the battlefield, get excited! When you are fighting God's fights, you want to be there, with His weapons in your hands and His power in your heart.

I was reading *USA Today* during the beginning of the recent war with Iraq. The newspaper gave accounts of the first Americans to die. My heart was moved as I looked at their pictures—men who gave their lives to protect me and my family and our future. Then I saw a picture that was too much for me—a ten-year-old African American boy, the son of one of those soldiers. He was holding the picture of his dad and standing at attention. He was saluting his father.

I lost it. This brave young boy would never have the chance to experience what my children share with me. Never again. I wanted to do something about it. I was angry. I wanted to head to Iraq and join the fight!

Realistically, though, it seemed there was nothing I could do. But then I heard the quiet, strong whisper of the Spirit of God: "Yes, John, there is something you can do. Be a father worthy of your own son's salute. And by the way, My son, don't forget that I died *for you*. Do I have *your* salute?"

He is the risen Commander, moving forward to victory. He beckons to all who follow Him to salute Him. When we do, we can expect to win. Whatever battle you are called to in this life, you can fight it with confidence and passion. Follow the Commander and charge! It's your privilege to be at the heart of the war.

chapter seven

A PROMISE TO GIVE AWAY

"To him be glory in the church and in Christ Jesus..."

THE PASSION PROMISE offers you a life that only God can imagine. It delivers you from boredom. But here's where we have to be careful. If we think that the promise is about *us*, we miss the whole point and the promise loses its power. To *Him* be glory. It's all about God!

Let's look again at Ephesians 3:20–21:

> Now to him who is able to do immeasurably more than all we ask or imagine, according to his power that is at work within us, to him be glory in the church and in Christ Jesus throughout all generations, for ever and ever! Amen.

Remember that as well as being an incredible promise in itself, this passage is also a doxology. It ascribes praise and glory to God. In fact, the word *doxology* comes from the Greek *doxa,* which is the word for *glory* in this passage. Our life becomes the adventure God intends only when we live it for His glory.

What is glory, anyway? The word means "to recognize someone for who he really is." If we give God glory, it means we live in full recognition of who He is. Our life will reflect who He is as He lives in us. And it will be quite a life—not because of us, but because of the One in us.

In Scripture, glory follows Jesus everywhere He goes. We see "the glory of the Lord" shining when His birth is announced (Luke 2:9). Almost every time we hear of His return, we learn that He "comes in his glory" (Matthew 25:31; Luke 9:26). In fact, Paul says that He is "the Lord of glory" (1 Corinthians 2:8).

Glory characterizes all that Christ is and all that He does. Glory is the "shining forth" of the very essence of God. Paul says, "So whether you eat or drink or *whatever you do,* do it all for the glory of God" (1 Corinthians 10:31). Whatever you do.

The purpose of our life is to love the Lord, to bring Him glory, and to display His glory in the world. It is only with this desire burning in us that we can truly live out the Passion Promise. It is impossible to give Him glory and at the same time keep His glory to ourselves. The Passion Promise is a promise to give away.

Remember—a person of authentic passion *intentionally shares genuine passion.* Glory is found "in Christ Jesus," and Jesus can always be found touching lives and sharing the glory of God in ways that even the outcasts can experience for themselves.

GLORY IN THE CHURCH?

Glory is also to be found "in the church." But these days the glory of God is noticeably absent in the church. When you see the glory of God among people in the Bible, they fall on their faces or break out in worship or rejoice with the angels or see thousands saved in a day. Is that happening in your church? In your life? If not, why?

Everyone will see the glory of God when Jesus returns. Why make them wait? The world ran to the New Testament church, but runs away from ours. It's time to give people a reason to run back!

Kris has been running away from a "gloryless" church for a long time. I met her while working on this book. She waited on me and some friends at a steak restaurant. I'm not sure I've ever met someone so antagonistic toward Christians. When she heard that I was a pastor, she was openly scornful about Christianity. She nearly ran away when we prayed over the food and actually asked us *not* to pray for her.

Later, Kris told us that she had studied all the world religions and grew up in a very strict church, but had had her fill of "religious hypocrites." Her parents' becoming Aryan Nation leaders probably hadn't helped much. Kris angrily listed the many experiences she'd been through with "religious" people. As she walked away from the table, she said, "I have no use for religion at all."

I said, "Kris, I agree with you 100 percent."

She stopped in her tracks and looked at me as if I were insane. "How can you be a pastor and not be religious?"

I told her that it was the religious people that hated Jesus the most and that what had changed my life was a relationship, not a religion.

Kris looked puzzled and walked away. But the next time she came to our table, everything in her countenance had changed. She sat down and said, "Tell me more about this." I shared with her the personal love and glory of Jesus that she could know for herself. She agreed to continue the dialogue by mail and gave me her address. It was obvious that this young woman had never had the slightest glimpse of the glory of God. She had no idea who Jesus was.

Just before writing this today, I had lunch with some new friends in Orlando. This wonderful couple told me that they had lived in the Atlanta area, where I live, for eight years and had never known an active Christian. No one had shared Jesus with them. No one ever invited them to church. They were sitting at an Atlanta Braves game one day and saw someone holding a sign that said "John 3:16." She asked her husband what it meant. They didn't know!

How many believers were sitting around them that day who could have told them? How many of them shouted at the top of their lungs for the Braves but wouldn't even whisper the name of Jesus to someone who desperately needed to hear it? Thankfully, this family moved to Florida and met some Christians. Today they are faithful followers of the Savior that no one in Atlanta would tell them about.

I find this couple's experience to be more the norm than the exception. How can this be? Because so few churches, or individual believers for that matter, ever live out the glory of God for anyone in the world to see.

Vance Havner writes, "The church suffers today from a saddening lack of old-fashioned, simple-hearted, overflowing Christian joy. We have plenty of knowledge, plenty of enthusiasm and denominational zeal, but Christians and churches that started out in revival fires are living in the smoke."[7]

I don't know about you, but I don't want to live all my life in a smoky fog where the glory of God is nothing more than dying embers. It's time for some fresh fires to burn. I want to see His glory! I want to see what happens when the world sees it, too.

So how do we go about lighting those fires? How do we move from being firefighters to fire*lighters*? How do we see the glory of God again in our churches and our lives? I believe that God longs to show His glory to and through His people. He is not stingy with His glory. But He is careful with it. He won't entrust His glory to those He knows will misuse it.

My daughters are the joy of my life. I know the day approaches when into each of their lives will come a young man who will treasure them as I do. But if a convicted felon shows up at my door, dirty, smelling bad, a cigarette in one hand and a beer in the other, do you think I'm going to say, "Well, hi there! Let me go get my daughter"? No, I'm more likely to go get my gun!

I'm not putting what is precious to me into the hands of someone who cannot be trusted. Neither will God. And His glory is precious to Him. It is His essence, His shining forth, the core of His nature. He says, "I am the LORD; that is my name! I will not give my glory to another" (Isaiah 42:8).

The key question is, can you be trusted with God's glory? Can God trust your church with His glory? God stands ready to pour out His glory. He wants to! The glory of God can return to you, and to your church, if you rely on Him to make it happen.

But what exactly is God looking for? When the glory of God returns, where does it go?

GOD'S GLORY RETURNS TO REPENTANT HEARTS

God makes it clear that the loss of His glory among His people is our responsibility. God Himself seems to be amazed that we would trade His glory for anything else:

> "My people have exchanged their Glory for worthless idols. Be appalled at this, O heavens, and shudder with great horror," declares the LORD. "My people have committed two sins: They have forsaken me, the spring of living water, and have dug their own cisterns, broken cisterns that cannot hold water." (Jeremiah 2:11–13)

That is precisely where so many of us are—trapped in our own cisterns, stuck in a gloryless life and a gloryless church. But it doesn't have to stay that way!

We're never far from His glory. Scripture says, "Surely his salvation is near those who fear him, that his glory may dwell in our land" (Psalm 85:9). The Bible is the story of sinful people repenting, returning to God, and experiencing His love, grace, and glory again and again. It all begins with repentance—a return to God, seeking forgiveness for going our own ways.

God always responds to repentance. And then the glory begins to return. Isaiah said of his sinful people, "The Redeemer will come to Zion, to those in Jacob who repent of their sins" (Isaiah 59:20).

And what is the result of repentance? Listen to the next verses in Isaiah:

> "Arise, shine, for your light has come, and the glory
> of the LORD rises upon you. See, darkness covers the
> earth and thick darkness is over the peoples, but the
> LORD rises upon you and his glory appears over you.
> Nations will come to your light, and kings to the
> brightness of your dawn." (Isaiah 60:1–3)

Wow! When God's glory shines again, it can't be missed. Nations and kings notice.

Does this seem a little far-fetched, the idea that something could happen in your life or church that would catch the attention of nations and kings? Well, it's not. It has happened several times before. Historians call these times spiritual awakenings—great movements of God that change not just believers, but whole cultures and nations. You may not have read much about this in your history books in school, but our own country was born out of a great spiritual awakening. (Check out *Firefall* by Alvin Reid and Malcolm McDow for a full study of these movements.)

All of the great movements of God originate with repentance. Let *your* repentant heart be the start of such a movement as you are trusted with the glory of God.

GOD'S GLORY RETURNS TO THOSE WHO SHARE IT

I believe that one of the quickest and most powerful ways to light fresh fires of God's glory is to begin investing in relationships with unbelievers like Kris. If you want to see glory, you have to see Jesus. If you want to see Jesus, just look for the lost, and there He'll be! Jesus said it Himself: "The Son of Man came to seek and to save what was lost" (Luke 19:10).

There has never been a war like the one fought in 2003 in Iraq. I was amazed to see the live bullet-by-bullet account of the war on the news. Americans have never been exposed so clearly and directly to the horrors of war. When the first American casualties began being reported, I sensed a real sadness in our land and in my own heart. As I reflected on what was happening, however, a thought hit me: *Far more people will die in America today than in Iraq.*

These people won't die because of firefights and bombs but from heart attacks, cancer, old age, and a whole array of other causes. Yet they will be just as dead as those killed in the war. They will stand before the same God.

And their deaths will barely affect us.

It often takes something like a war to remind us of the reality and the preciousness of the life we have. But it *must* affect us if we want to see the glory of God again. The ultimate expression of the Passion Promise is to follow Jesus to someone He loves and to see that person experience the Passion Promise for himself. It doesn't get any better! When introducing others to Jesus becomes central in your life, that's when you will really know the fullness of God's passion. For when you share His promise with others, He will multiply it in your own life. That's the way He works.

Many at the church I pastor are starting to get this. They have come to believe that it is our incredible privilege to love people—especially those who don't know Jesus' love. God is honoring their desire to show His glory to others.

Several in my church began to share a friendship with an Islamic man in our community I'll call Ahmed. Ahmed owns a business in our city and Ray, Darla, Dave, Marsha, Charles, Bonnie, and Lucy, among others, made it a point to consistently demonstrate love to him.

At first Ahmed was resistant, saying he would tell any "preacher" that tried to talk to him about Jesus to go to hell. Over time, however, he became curious about what made these people care the way they did. He even started to call one couple from our church "Mom and Pop."

One day Ahmed said to the couple, "Some people tell me your church is a cult."

"Why do they think that?" Ray asked.

"Because of the way you love people! It's not normal. It's different from other religions. I believe you would love me even if I never became a Christian."

Soon Ahmed and I began having lunch together. He became my friend. Sitting at lunch one afternoon, Ahmed asked me how he could really know that Jesus was God. I sensed it was one of those Passion Promise moments, so I stepped way out on a limb (actually it felt more like I was falling off of it) and said, "Well, let's ask Him to show you before lunch is finished."

"You're kidding," he said.

Before I could change my mind, I bowed my head and asked Jesus to show Ahmed that He was real—that He was God—before we finished lunch. Ahmed started looking around, as if wondering if He might really show up!

A server named Teresa brought our food. I asked her if I could pray about anything for her. She seemed amazed that I would be interested in praying for her and sat right down with us. She poured out a miserable story of broken relationships and her desire to end her life the night before. "I don't know why I didn't do it," she said.

"I know why," I said. "God had an appointment for you. You needed to meet us today." Since her shift was almost over, I invited her to join us when she was ready.

When Teresa returned, I asked if she had ever been to church. She said that she had gone to that big church up the road for a Christmas show one time. She was talking about my church! She said she cried through the whole service. I asked why she'd never come back. Don't miss what she said. It's what many unchurched people think.

"On a Sunday?" Teresa said. "Oh no. That's when good people go to church. I'm not a good person."

I told her that she had misunderstood Jesus, that He loved her just like she was, and that He could change her and come into her life.

"Right here in the restaurant?" she asked.

Before I could answer, Ahmed said, "Do it, Teresa, do it!

I'm not even a Christian, but I know these people will love you like no one else ever will!"

A few moments later Teresa was my sister in Christ. It was sure the first time a Muslim helped me lead anyone to Jesus!

That Sunday, Ahmed and his wife brought Teresa to church. Do you know what it was like for all those who had loved and shared with Ahmed to see him at church with a new believer he helped lead to Jesus? It was overwhelming! Do you think I have to work very hard to stir up passion in those people's lives? They're passion factories!

Just a few months ago Ahmed began having dreams and visions of Jesus calling to him. After two hours of talking in a Cracker Barrel restaurant, we sat in his truck and Ahmed became my brother in Christ. He now meets me and other men at 5:45 on Monday mornings as he learns how to follow Jesus and prepares for the day when he will openly share with his family the decision he has made. I get excited all over again just writing about it.

This is passion beyond belief, lives changed forever, the return of the glory of God. Get in on it!

GOD'S GLORY RETURNS WHEN PASSION LEADERS LEAD

Have you noticed that God does very little of significance in the Bible without first recruiting a human leader? He certainly doesn't need us to accomplish His plan—but we *are* His plan. He doesn't have a plan B or C. We're it.

When God is ready to move, He moves through people and He invites leaders to lead—people with a passion for His passion who will follow Him and lead others to do the same. Are you interested? Then let's look at what I consider to be the best one-verse picture of leadership in the Bible.

Recently my wife told me that God had led her to a Scripture she believed was His verse to me for the year. My wife is very discerning. I have learned to listen to her when she shares something like this with me. That was a good decision, for this passage has impacted me deeply. It is what I want to be and what I hope you want to be.

It's a picture of a leader named David: "And David shepherded them with integrity of heart; with skillful hands he led them" (Psalm 78:72). I believe that within this verse are the three essential ingredients for becoming one of God's passion leaders—ingredients that you and I need.

A Calling

David was a shepherd. But it was more than what he did; it was who he was. From childhood he did it. He took it seriously. The flock was his family livelihood. You were an unfortunate wolf or lion if you came after David's sheep!

David carried this identity with him to the throne of Israel. Though he became a king, in his heart he was still a shepherd caring for his flock. It's what he was *born* to do.

What were you born to do? Do you know? Why did God put you here? What are you uniquely gifted for, passionate about, prepared for? That's your calling. God gives everyone a purpose for this life. As Bruce Wilkinson writes in *The Dream Giver*, "You have been handcrafted by God to accomplish a part of His Big Dream for the world.... No one else can do it quite like you."[8]

If you don't know God's purpose for you, you'd better find out. Quickly!

How do you find out? Well, you know what you're passionate about. You know how God has prepared you. Ask someone you trust to be honest with you about what gifts they see in you. Take a spiritual gifts inventory or a course designed to help you find your calling. Put all that together and ask God to speak clearly to you.

Don't wait! Life is short. It's a tragedy to miss why you are really here. Find your calling and you will have the passion you need to be a passion leader.

Character

David had integrity of heart. People wanted to follow him. They trusted him. And when he failed, sometimes miserably, he took responsibility and moved on, forgiven by God and better for the experience. That's character!

Character is desperately needed today. In fact, it is so rare that almost anywhere real character shows up, people come to see it—and to follow. You don't have to possess the most charismatic personality or the most brilliant mind. In fact, many of the greatest leaders seem to have very "ordinary" personalities and intellects.

One of the few business books I have ever insisted that our staff read is *Good to Great* by Jim Collins. In his study, Collins found that the companies that went from being good companies to great companies were without exception led by unassuming servant-leaders who did not have charismatic or magnetic personalities. What these leaders did have was character. Everyone around them knew it and respected and followed them because of it.

Pursue character and you will be a leader.

Competence

Leaders like David have skillful hands. They are committed to excellence and will not settle for less. In fact, God may withhold His glory from many of us because He knows we will be lazy with it. That's inexcusable! Christians should do things with greater excellence than anyone because we know who we are doing it for! Remember—we "do it all for the glory of God" (1 Corinthians 10:31).

A new believer recently told me that before he met Christ he'd never had much contact with Christians. They didn't spend time doing the things he was involved in. I assumed he meant alcohol, drugs, or something similar. He said, "No, I mean in the highest levels of business success."

That really troubled me. I believe that the best cars, toys, games, movies, music, food, and everything else should be made by Christians. We're doing it for His glory!

I was able to teach a great leadership lesson to my son the other day. Trey runs for his middle school track team. I picked him up at school one afternoon, and as we drove by the track we saw a high school student running alone.

Trey said, "That guy is incredible! He's like the state champion in everything!"

"Why do you think he's so good, Trey?" I asked.

"I don't know, Dad."

"Why aren't you at track practice?"

"We didn't have it today," he said.

"Did the high school team have practice?"

"No."

As we watched that one lonely runner continue around the track, I said, "I guess we know now why he's so good."

Will you commit yourself to becoming the very best you can be at what God has given you a passion to do—what you were born for? Will you do it with integrity of heart? Then you will be a leader that God can trust with His glory.

TWO ASSIGNMENTS

I want to give you two assignments that will launch you into the joy of the Passion Promise, into the heat of the battle, and into the middle of His glory.

First, refuse to limit your spiritual experience to people who look like you. One of the hallmarks of the New Testament church was that they demolished the walls of racial division. One of the hallmarks of our churches is that we have built them right back up again.

I can't think of a clearer or more powerful way to see the glory of God than for the church to solve the problems our government has utterly failed to solve. Isn't that what the church was meant to do? To be the salt and the light of this world? If your community is racially diverse and your church is not, can you really tell God that you are reaching your community? And if you're not reaching your community, what's your excuse?

Our church had almost no African Americans in attendance a few years ago. The neighborhood closest to our church was entirely black, yet no one from that neighborhood had even visited New Hope. We knew we had to somehow make it known that everyone was welcome at our church.

So we got intentional. We decided to find out what it took to reach African Americans, not because they were black, but because they were our neighbors and we were having no impact on their lives at all. We were criticized by some for "targeting" a particular race. That still puzzles me. I sure am glad that Paul, a Jew, targeted Gentiles or I'd be going to hell right now!

Today we have many African American families in our church, and more are coming every week. We're having a great time. We're learning that we are stronger together than apart. We are crossing into each other's cultures and watching new bonds of love grow that never existed before. This is New Testament Christianity.

But we can't be naive. Taking God's glory to the world isn't easy. It *is* easy to stay the same, to ignore those who are different from us, to keep the boat from rocking. But spreading the name of Jesus is challenging. It's different. It's beyond our comfort zones. It's out on the edge. But that's where the glory is!

If we are willing to go out on that ledge and address the real problems of our culture, such as the racial divide, with the life-changing passion of Jesus, then the world will see His glory again.

TAKE IT OUTSIDE

Here's my second assignment for you: Be part of taking His glory outside of your own country. With all God has given us in the American church, can you think of one good excuse we can offer for not taking His message to everyone on this planet? I promise you this—if you will leave your home, even if only for a few weeks, and go to another culture with the love of Jesus, you will see more of the Passion Promise than you will know what to do with.

New Hope was a wonderful church when I became its pastor seven years ago. They were ready for a big leap forward in touching the world. Not long after I arrived, I took a small group from our church to a former Soviet republic that I had visited many times before. I had been invited to speak at a military base—by an agnostic colonel. He said I could speak only about morals, not about Jesus. I had no idea how to do that.

On the way to the base, we stopped to pick up the colonel, a short, muscular man with a piercing stare. I soon realized that he was mad as a hornet. As he talked, our interpreter began to smile. "Good news!" he said. "The KGB is coming to hear you preach today!"

That didn't sound like good news at all to me. The KGB was still very powerful in this republic; it wasn't uncommon for people to disappear. How could this be good news?

"The colonel hates the KGB," the interpreter explained. "He says now you can preach about anything you want."

What a day that was. I preached the gospel to the KGB and the soldiers at that former Soviet military base. At the end I gave an invitation, and hundreds accepted Christ—including the colonel! Over the next few years we prayed often for him. At one point we heard he had been arrested for his faith, but was then miraculously restored to his position. We had to go back and check it out.

When we got there, we couldn't believe what we saw. The colonel had transformed the military base into a lighthouse for the kingdom of God! Every soldier had a Bible; they worshiped together every Sunday; the colonel was up before dawn every day memorizing Scripture. They had a room set aside as a prayer chapel. There was a woodworking shop where the soldiers carved beautiful Scripture plaques in their spare time. They actually had billboards all over the base with the Word of God written on them.

The colonel ran to me and kissed me on both cheeks and called me brother. My fourteen-year-old daughter, Amy, was with me, and he even wanted to arrange a marriage for her with his son (that didn't go over so well with Amy).

The colonel and I spent a long time sharing and praying together. I said to my new friend, "Colonel, I'm worried about you. What you're doing could get you in trouble again with your government."

Without hesitation, the colonel said, "I am His soldier. I serve Jesus now!"

I still see him in my mind's eye. I see the place he has won in my heart. But most of all, I see the joy and passion of our common Lord that radiates from his face.

Only God can do something like that. No one who was there will ever forget it. The Passion Promise was no longer a sermon to hear in church. We were living it.

You can, too! You have a promise to give away. And when you do, it will come back to you again and again.

To Him be glory in the church and in Christ Jesus—and in you.

chapter eight

BRINGING THE
PASSION HOME

"Throughout all generations..."

HE MOST EXCITING thing on the face of this
earth is a family committed to following the Lord together. If
knowing that God has designed each of us for a life of passion is exciting for just one believer, how much more should
it mean to a family that can share in His passion and multiply it through their children and grandchildren?

Scripture speaks to the possibility and power of extend-
ing God's love and passion from one generation to the next:
"Know therefore that the LORD your God is God; he is the
faithful God, keeping his covenant of love to *a thousand generations* of those who love him and keep his commands"
(Deuteronomy 7:9). I don't want to be the one to break the

chain of God's covenant of love in my family!

I've been married to the most wonderful woman in the world for twenty-three years. We learned a long time ago that God's plan for our marriage is often an absolute adventure. But sometimes things get too exciting.

During the Christmas season of 2001, the annual day of terror had come—putting up the Christmas lights. My decorating misadventures had resulted in many memorable moments, but this year took the prize.

I stretched the lights out on the driveway and plugged them in to see if any were out. To my great frustration I found that *none* of the strings worked. I noticed several broken bulbs that were causing the problem, and forgetting that the lights were still plugged in, I started to pull on one of the broken bulbs. At that moment, my barefoot wife came outside and walked across the damp concrete. Smiling, Donna said, "Thanks so much for doing this, honey," and gave me a kiss.

The next few moments were pretty unusual. I was knocked to the ground by the jolt, and my wife was jolted loose from our electric lip-lock, shouting, "I've been shocked!"

Inside the house, my son thought Donna was yelling "I've been shot!" He came running out with his pocketknife to protect his mother. Meanwhile, I recovered my senses and stumbled to my feet, thinking, *Wow, that woman can kiss!*

Now *that's* an exciting marriage.

Of course, our marriages *should* be exciting. That's how God planned it. And that excitement should be shared. When Paul wrote "throughout all generations" in his prayer for the Ephesians, He meant that a father and mother must pass on their passion for a life designed by God to their children, and then those children must do the same with their own sons and daughters, like a mountain stream that keeps flowing and spreading wider into the valleys below.

The Passion Promise was at work in my family long before I was even born. I am blessed beyond measure by my family heritage. I had wonderful grandparents and an incredible mother and father. My dad gave our family a wonderful gift when he compiled all of his notes on the Gospel of John into a book. Throughout the book, Dad shares personal insights from his life. Here is a small part of his story:

> I was named John Paul, the son of Olin Avant. At age thirteen, during revival services at First Methodist Church in Wetumpka, Alabama, my name was changed to Paul, a believer and follower of Jesus Christ. I didn't understand it all then and not fully even now. But I know for sure that real life for me began that day. I became a "new babe" in Christ. I see today that my life was totally different afterward than what the world around me expected.
>
> *Unexpected and unexplainable things began to happen in my life that day!* It wasn't that I was doing things differently. It was that He was doing things differently in me! I look back at it now and I know that He prepared me for that time. My heart was ready. My decision was sincere. My desires began to align more closely with His desires. He revealed real Truth, which is Jesus Christ, to me. I found Jesus after He found me with a seeking and open heart. Life has never been the same since.

Can you feel the passion in my father's words? In his life? Now I have the privilege of handing down that passion for Christ to my own children. The wonderful part is that I don't have to do it alone—I get to share it with my parents as well. And one day I hope to help my son and daughters pass it on to their children.

A TREASURE FOR GENERATIONS

My son and I have a "treasure chest" that my dad made for us. Inside it we put things that are significant to us as father and son. The first thing that went in the treasure chest was a note from my dad to be passed on to the generations ahead:

> Son, grandson, great- and great-great-grandson, future generations—listen to me! Choose Jesus Christ! He stands at the door and knocks and weeps when you turn away. I can only pass along to you my testimony and my heritage of faith in Jesus Christ. It is your responsibility to choose for yourself. Your choice will have eternal consequences for you and your children after you. I pray that not a single one of you will break the chain of our family serving the Lord until the end of the age when Jesus calls His whole family home to the place He is preparing.

I realize that a family legacy like this is exceedingly rare and precious. But why should it be so unusual? Why shouldn't God's people expect to live this way—if not to continue a wonderful legacy, at least to start one?

Even if you are single or don't have children, you have a role to play in spreading God's passion "throughout all generations." I believe that the collapse of the family today requires *every believer* to have an impact on the life of a child. Opportunities are everywhere. For example, instead of coming to church Wednesday nights, my wife joins several other New Hope women—some without kids at home—and takes church to a juvenile detention center, where they are helping a group of girls learn what it means to be women.

Lee Haney, an eight-time Mr. Olympia, is a member of our church and has a ministry to boys without dads called Haney's Harvest House. One of our men was spending time with one of the boys recently and was playing Christian music. Listening to a song about the Lord, the little boy said, "Hey, who is Jesus anyway?"

Shouldn't *every* little boy and girl have a chance to know about Jesus? Whether we're single, married, have a houseful of children, or are childless, we have to help them get that chance. Some child you've never met may *need* you. You can show that child love and a passion for Jesus that he or she might never find anywhere else.

Do you see the opportunity? You and future generations can show the world a life only God can imagine, right up to the moment Jesus returns! If you have children, or if you ever plan to, I want you to discover an awesome sense of destiny as you think about what this can mean for your children.

There has never been a better time for believers to follow their destiny. Christian families are in deep trouble today. Upon leaving home, 80 percent or more of our children almost immediately leave the church.[9] It seems that because we parents view our faith only as a Sunday ritual, modeling a weak imitation of genuine Christianity, our children abandon their faith as soon as they don't have to go to church with Mom and Dad. This has to change! We must become parents and families of *authentic* passion, rejecting imitation passion.

What if we did pass on a life of passion to our children as the absolute heart and soul of what our faith is all about? What if our children grew up *expecting* to see God at work in every step of their lives? What if they saw His power from the time they could speak? What if they grasped the truth that a life so powerful awaited them that only God could have imagined it?

Think about it—what if our children realized that God would be life itself to them, that His power would always be enough, and that they could know Him intimately every moment of all their days?

Are these enough reasons for you to bring passion for God and His plan home to your family? Then let's talk about how to make it happen.

MODELING PASSION AT HOME

Before you can teach your children how to live a life of passion for God, you must live it out in front of them. They need to hear you and your spouse praying together. They need to see how excited you are about what God is doing in your lives. They need to watch as you develop relationships with passion partners. They need to see your joy as you share your faith with others. Most of all, they need to see that you are real. This generation of young people is desperate for authentic relationship. If they see it in Mom and Dad, they will want what you have.

This may sound like a dramatic change for your family. It may even sound impossible. I wish I could offer you a short-cut, but there isn't one. I simply ask you this: What would you be willing to change, how much would you sacrifice, if your legacy could be a group of children who change the world?

That's what is possible. That's what is at stake.

So start where you are. If your spouse is willing, read this book together and commit to a course of action. Develop an ongoing strategy for modeling a passionate life for God as a way of life to your family. It takes time and effort to plan your finances, to set goals for your job, even to improve your golf game. Will you not invest time in this for your children, for their future?

Be patient with yourselves. Don't expect perfection. Just get started. Make the changes you need to make in your lives and marriage, and start today. If your spouse won't partici-pate, model a passionate, godly life for your children by yourself. Don't be surprised, though, if your spouse sees the changes in you and begins to change, too! After all, the Passion Promise is contagious.

DISCOVER EVERYDAY PASSION

I believe you need a two-pronged strategy for teaching your children. First, you need a plan to model the passionate life for them in the normal course of your everyday lives. Identify the times you already spend together as a family. Do you have breakfast together? Dinners at home? Do you go out to a restaurant on the weekend? Take advantage of these opportunities. If you don't have such times, you need to change your schedule immediately. When your family is too busy to be together, you are headed for trouble or you are already there.

What do you do with the time you spend together? Help your children understand the excitement of how God really works. If they think church is boring, they may begin to believe that God is boring. Tell them stories from this book and from the Bible, or tell them the stories of what God is doing with you and in the lives of your friends. Encourage your children to begin watching for God to work in unusual ways and to tell you about it.

Pray with your family! Pray at meals; set a time for regular brief family devotions. Share what God is saying to you and how you are growing to know Him as the personal and passionate God. Pray privately with your children before they go to bed, even when they are older. Take that time to talk to them and find out what God is doing in their lives.

Recently I asked four hundred men to raise their hands if they had heard their fathers pray out loud with them other than when blessing their food. Only fourteen hands went up. What a sad statement! We fathers must change this pattern, starting with our own children.

While you're teaching your children that God offers them a life of passion, remember that they will be confronted daily with every imaginable imitation and alternative. As they get older and more set in their ways, it will become even harder for them to choose well. So talk openly with them about the imitations they will face. You know what's coming!

You have a wonderful alternative to just telling your children, "Don't do that." Instead, tell them why not to do it—because whatever calls to them is a pathetic whine compared to the mighty roar of God's authentic, exciting passion for them.

As a family, identify some impossible situations that God wants you to enter into so He can show you His power. Pray about these situations, and then watch your children's faith and excitement about who God really is grow as He answers. This gives God a chance to teach your children that a person of authentic passion lives each day *expecting* passion.

Several years ago our own family faced a choice. We had saved some money and now were ready to either spend it on a car we "had" to have or commit it to a new building fund at our church. Donna and I felt God leading us to use this as an opportunity to show our children the way He works. We began giving the money to the church. At the same time, our leased car was nearing its time to be returned to the dealer.

We waited and prayed with our children. When they asked what we would do without a car, we said that we would get to see God provide. And He did! Just before the lease was up on our car, a dealer offered to let me drive demos for free. We did that for almost the entire three years of the church building program. Our family was able to rejoice in the way our God works in our lives—and our kids learned a big lesson.

These are just some suggestions. You can come up with many of your own. Just be sure that whatever you do gives God the opportunity to show your children how exciting it is to live a life only He can imagine.

CREATE SPECIAL MOMENTS

The second part of the two-pronged strategy for your family is to create life-changing moments for each of your children. These moments must be designed to teach your kids how to live the life only God can imagine for them. This takes planning, time, and money, but it is vitally important and the rewards are incredible.

Two experiences have been absolutely life-changing for our children. First, we take special trips during which the men in our family teach the boys how to passionately follow Jesus. We call this group the Knights of Adventure, and it consists of my father, brother, and brother-in-law, and our sons. We camp out for two nights and ask God to show us His power. (Be sure to read the wonderful book *How to Raise a Modern-Day Knight* by Robert Lewis for extensive help in putting together these kinds of outings.)

A few years ago, in front of our boys, we asked God to show us His real power while we were on our campout. What a chance for our passionate God to reveal who He really was to a group of boys watching to see Him work! He didn't let us down.

My son had turned ten that year, and we had a ceremony in which I gave him a gold-bladed Buck knife. He was an excited young man! A piece of paper fell out of the box the knife had been in. We could hardly believe what we read. It was a note from the president of the company, Chuck Buck, sharing the good news of Jesus Christ with anyone who bought his knives. We read the note and stood wide-eyed with our boys as we celebrated that wonderful moment.

But God wasn't finished.

The next day, on our way home, Trey and I went on a pilgrimage to the Bass Pro Shop—a huge hunting and fishing store, heaven on earth for men and boys. We were walking around looking at all the great stuff when we heard an announcement: "For the next fifteen minutes come meet Chuck Buck at the Buck knife counter."

I looked in my son's eyes and saw the passion I was looking for. He knew that his God was real—and was working right where he was! He had revealed His power to us just like we had asked Him to.

When we saw Chuck Buck, I said, "Have we got a story for you." Moved by what we told him, he engraved his signature on the blade of Trey's new knife. My son now sleeps with that knife next to his bed.

When you and your family pile up memories like these over the years, you'll raise sons and daughters who will walk right into a life only God can imagine.

Our family has also committed to taking each of our kids on a mission trip before they become teenagers. Nothing we have done has been as important in the lives of our children. I want them to get out of their comfort zones and see God work in ways they cannot imagine in their own culture. This experience has changed each of them forever.

In 1994, when my daughter Christi was ten, we went to Belarus in the former Soviet Union. One day as we preached at the marketplace, hundreds of people left the food lines to listen because they were even hungrier for the bread of life. When I finished speaking, crowds of people accepted Christ.

It was then that we made a big mistake. We told the

people that we had Bibles but that we didn't have enough for everyone. Before we could say another word, a near riot broke out as people scrambled to grab Bibles out of boxes. They ripped and tore and wrestled for each copy.

My daughter became frightened as people pushed and shoved. She shouted, "Daddy, get more Bibles! There aren't enough!"

I told her we didn't have any more, and she began to cry.

At the edge of the crowd stood an old woman. She was too feeble to enter this frenzy, but she was shouting and waving her hands. We could hear her scream, *"Pashalzta!"*—"Please!" I had one Bible that I had stuck in my coat for safekeeping. I walked to the old woman with my daughter and an interpreter. She told us her story through her tears.

This woman was one of the few in the crowd that day who was already a believer. She had been raised in an evangelical home, but the last time she had seen a Bible was when she was young. Stalin's soldiers had come for her father and had taken him and the family Bible away. She never saw either again.

As she continued to cry, the woman said, "I thought that before I died I was going to be able to have God's Word again, but I missed it." One of the greatest privileges of my life was to place that last Bible in her hands. She kissed me and gave me flowers and walked away shouting, *"Slava Bogu!"*—"Praise God!"

That day my daughter decided she would be God's radical, that she would follow Him passionately and make a difference in this world. She has never turned from that course. She is now a sophomore at Palm Beach Atlantic

University studying musical theater. She has this crazy belief that God has a life for her bigger than she can dream. So she is setting her sights on New York City and hopes to see Broadway changed by the power of her Lord.

What a thrill it is to see your children realize that they *can* live a life only God can imagine!

SHOW YOUR PASSION—FOR BETTER AND FOR WORSE

Don't hide your battles from your children. Donna and I decided early in our marriage that we would not hide our arguments from our children. We would let them see us fuss, get angry, get over it, and make up. We believed then, and still believe, that this allows them to see how real life works and to be secure that Mom and Dad can get upset without leaving each other.

Our kids have gotten so used to this that sometimes when we are arguing, they'll say something like, "Why don't you just make up now and get it over with?"

When you are wounded, let them know. When you are discouraged and struggling, let them see it. If tragedy comes, let them grieve with you. Your children will learn that God is authentic and relevant even in their deepest needs. They will watch as your faith passes the test, and theirs will grow stronger.

Don't try to shield your kids from their own battles. Help them follow Jesus passionately through them. And teach them to care when others hurt. Throughout the church are families who have been through every conceivable fire and have found Jesus to be more than enough. Go to lunch with these people. Let your children see how the God you serve enters into real needs.

One of the great blessings of parenthood comes when your children begin living a passionate life in such a way that *they* minister to *you*. I still cherish the memory of one of those blessings.

It began with me standing in the kitchen, trying to think of some way not to go out the door to the airport. I was headed to a dangerous country on a long mission trip, and I didn't want to go. I felt tired and lonely, and I hadn't even left my family yet. For some reason this mission trip just didn't seem right. Had I missed God?

My wife placed an envelope in my hand. "Read this on the plane," she said. "It's from Christi." And she kissed me good-bye.

Depressed and discouraged, I took my seat on the plane, settled in for a fourteen-hour flight, and opened the envelope. Inside was something that rekindled the fire in my heart for living out God's plan for me. Here is what I read:

> My favorite poem is "The Road Not Taken" by Robert Frost. The last three lines say: "Two roads diverged in a wood and I—I took the one less traveled by. And that has made all the difference." What a difference it has made in our family's life! You're in for this awesome adventure only because you chose that road and never once have I seen you look back. You're my champion, my hero, and one of my best friends. I will pray for you every day, and because you have taken the road less traveled by, I will, too. Love, Christi.

I could give you a long list of all the things I have messed up as a dad or as a pastor. But this letter was evidence of something I'd done right. It is my treasure—not for sale at any price. Because just reading it every now and then reminds me that it is worth anything to live by the Passion Promise. Following Jesus' big dreams instead of my own is an incredible way to live. And to do it together as a family? It doesn't get any better.

So kiss your spouse tonight, hug your kids, thank God for your family, and bring the passion home with you. You and your family can make a difference—*throughout all generations!*

chapter nine

A PASSION TOO BIG
FOR THIS WORLD

"For ever and ever..."

Can you take me higher?
To the place where blind men see
Can you take me higher?
To the place with golden streets

*D*O THESE WORDS sound familiar? Maybe from an old revival hymn? A new worship chorus? Not quite. If you've heard them, it was probably on the radio. They're from a recent number one song called "Higher" by the rock band Creed.

The members of Creed say that they're not a Christian band and have a variety of beliefs. They record with a secular label and play in sold-out venues around the world. Many consider them the number one rock band today.

What's the secret to their appeal? First of all, they're very good (yes, I'm a fan). But I believe that their popularity goes much deeper. Creed has tapped into a spiritual hunger in the world today. They are speaking to hearts that are hungry for the eternal, for something that lasts and is bigger than they are; something that is real, that could actually be experienced beyond this life. Take a look at more of their lyrics:

> So let's go there
> > Let's make our escape
> Come on let's go there
> > Let's ask can we stay?

How ironic and sad it is that the world is talking about heaven and is hungry to know about eternity, yet the church rarely brings it up. Many Christian leaders have pointed out to me that pastors seem to think preaching about heaven is viewed as irrelevant by most people. These pastors believe if we are to reach people where they are, we must tell them how to succeed in life, how to handle relationships, how to raise their children. These things may be important, but if we think people today aren't interested in the eternal, we're completely out of touch.

In fact, we may be part of the most spiritually open society in centuries. Previous generations of secular people hesitated to believe anything, but members of this postmodern culture are willing to believe almost everything! The afterlife is big business today. If you can do a little parlor magic on television to communicate with dear deceased

Grandma, people will gladly make you a wealthy man.

Of course, it only makes sense for people to give great attention to eternity. After all, that's where they'll spend 99.9 percent of their lives! Believers understand that they will experience the joy of heaven after they die. Yet it has always puzzled me that so many Christians miss the message of the Passion Promise and live their earthly lives bored and unfulfilled.

It happens because they focus only on the temporary. They just don't get it. The framework for their lives has shrunk from the great adventure of Ephesians 3:20–21 down to "the stuff that has to get done today."

You won't ever really understand God's promise for your life if you limit it to this world. God's passion is too big for this world! Even the death of Jesus is called His "passion." Passion in this life is incomplete without understanding that it is fulfilled in the next.

C. S. Lewis believed that all the beautiful and good things we see on this earth are only shadows of reality in heaven. If our focus never goes beyond this life, we are destined to devote ourselves to shadows. Lewis said, "If I find in myself a desire which no experience in this world can satisfy, the most probable explanation is that I was made for another world."[10]

Wow! This is important—too important to miss. With all the wonder that living passionately for God brings to this earthly existence, it is only the beginning. You were made for another, more satisfying world.

So how should this affect our lives here? Should we just sit around and wait for the next world? Not even close! All that you experience of God here on earth matters for eternity.

The literal translation of Paul's words "for ever and ever" in Ephesians 3:21 is "the age of the ages." We need to begin thinking in terms of ages. We should wake up each morning and say, "Lord, today I am privileged to live in Your promise of a life that is significant. Help me to live this day to the fullest, while remembering that I am made for another world."

This balance is crucial to living a life of freedom. If you will begin to think eternally, there are at least three ways that you will be set free.

GOD WILL DELIVER YOU FROM FEAR

Fear is destructive for many people. One of the most damaging anxieties can be the fear of death.

The 2002 sniper shootings in the Washington, D.C., area proved that. Fear gripped the nation as a sniper roamed the area, killing people at random. People changed their lives in an attempt to stay out of harm's way—running from the malls to their cars, hiding while filling their cars with gas, canceling major events, staying in their homes. People knew that the odds of being shot by the sniper were far less than the chances of being killed in a car accident, but still they were afraid. Death suddenly felt random, very real, and frighteningly near.

But thinking eternally changes our perspective. Do we really believe that God loves us? That He will be our shield until it is time for us to meet Him? That when we die, we will go to the world for which we were made? If so, then we know we have the tools to handle our fears.

Jesus clearly tells us how to respond to anxieties: "Do not be afraid. I am the First and the Last. I am the Living One; I was dead, and behold I am alive *for ever and ever!*" (Revelation 1:17–18). We don't have to be afraid! Christ has already kicked death in the teeth. No matter what happens to us, Jesus is alive for ever and ever! He promises us that where He is, there we will be.

I was driving through western North Carolina recently, listening to a pastor on the radio telling a wonderful story. He had been called to the hospital because an elderly woman in his church was dying of heart failure. The doctor wanted the pastor to help him tell the woman that she was about to die.

When the pastor reached her bedside and asked her how she was, she said with a smile, "I'm just looking for a shallow place to cross, pastor!"

The doctor came in the room and told the woman that she likely wouldn't live twenty-four hours. He was stunned to hear the woman say, "Did you hear that, pastor? I'm going to see Jesus today! Today!" And she began to worship.

The doctor ran from the room, and the pastor found him in the hall crying. The doctor said, "Reverend, what does that woman believe? Because whatever she believes is real!"

He was right. But I didn't have to hear that story to know it. I have seen that passionate faith myself in the eyes of people on their deathbeds as they stared past the end of their earthly lives and into the eyes of Jesus.

I saw heaven in the eyes of my dear friend Willie just before he died of cancer. He and his wife, Betty, had become like adopted grandparents to our children. Willie taught me a lot about passion for God. It broke my heart to sit by his bed as he neared death. But he died well—as he had lived.

And I have seen the reality of the eternal even more clearly in Betty's life since Willie's death. She recently found out that Willie's best friend from high school was also dying. He had no one to care for him, so Betty volunteered. She sat by his side in the nursing home reading the Word, singing to him, preparing him for his journey.

In his last moments, Betty said, "Richard, you're about to go to heaven. Take the hand of Jesus and He'll lead you—and He's going to take you to see Willie, too!" He smiled, a tear rolled down his cheek, and he closed his eyes and left this earth.

How can a woman care for her dying husband and then turn around and do the same thing for his friend? Because eternity is real! Thinking eternally while you are here on earth gives meaning forever to all you do—and delivers you from fear.

GOD WILL DELIVER YOU FROM THE TYRANNY OF THE TRIVIAL

When you think eternally, you begin to put life into perspective. Yes, every day is filled with frustrations, but soon they won't matter. Yes, a hundred things demand our time each day, but what will really matter in a thousand years? Trivial things are part of life. They're not bad, but many live in bondage to them, as if they were the key to fulfillment. Thinking eternally removes you from the tyranny of the trivial and helps you to focus the majority of your time on the things that matter most.

Erma lived that way. People often ask me why I think God did such a wonderful work of revival in our church in

Texas. I believe it was because of Erma and a few others like her. Erma was dying. She had been very sick for a long time and was wasting away. Erma once told me, "When you know you are dying, you want to concentrate on using your time well. I want to use my time to pray." And so she did.

When our church was struggling, Erma prayed constantly for God to move. And He did. After revival broke out, I would go visit her. She was bedridden by this time.

"Where are you speaking this week?" she would ask. "Where are others speaking? I have nothing more important to do than pray, and I will pray the whole time you speak." She did. And I believe that her prayers are the reason that movement of His Spirit spread so far and so powerfully. Erma was free! Trivial things held no grip on her. She was free to concentrate her remaining time on what really mattered.

"Remaining time." We don't like that phrase much, do we? It reminds us too loudly of our mortality. But we all have it—"remaining time." Some more, some less. What if we chose to live like Erma *now* with all of our remaining time? It could be revolutionary.

When Erma prayed, she knew—really knew—that she was making a difference in *two worlds*. She had been delivered from the trivial and saw the power of God. Now she lives in the world she was made for—a place where one day we will join her.

GOD WILL DELIVER YOU FROM EVIL

Jesus taught us to pray for deliverance from evil in the Lord's Prayer, and then immediately reminded us that His kingdom and power and glory are *forever*. Every day we battle with evil. We face the temptation to sin and often fail. But the best people I have ever known, the people who seemed to have the greatest victory over evil in their lives, have been those who truly understood how short this life is—and how long the next one is.

The best example of this understanding I've ever seen was in a man named Paul Stewart. Paul was amazing. I've never known anyone with more things physically wrong. He had struggled with Parkinson's disease, diabetes, kidney failure, amputated toes, blindness, and strokes. Yet I've also never known anyone who walked with Jesus quite like Paul did. Evil seemed to have no grip on him at all. He loved life and was a great artist and a wonderful husband and father.

When he went to the hospital for dialysis treatments, Paul would share Christ with all the others hooked up to machines. He would smile as he reminded me that he had a captive audience. When he had a stroke, the doctors asked him to smile to see if his face was affected. "That's easy," Paul said, "I always smile because I'm always thinking of my Lord." Once, he had something to share with our congregation during a response time. He couldn't walk up the steps so he *crawled* up instead. People listened when Paul spoke!

On June 6, 2002, Paul called me. I asked him how he was.

"I'm doing great! And I'm having a stroke right now." I had never heard *those* sentences used together before. Paul told me he was about to go to the hospital but felt the need to talk to me before he went.

I did something then that I'd never done in my ministry. I sensed God telling me to tape the phone call, so without saying anything to Paul, I grabbed my dictation recorder and turned it on. What I recorded became his last words. Not long after, Paul lost his speech, then consciousness. He died at the hospital.

This tape became precious to me, and of course, even more so to his family. I listened to it again today. During our conversation, I asked Paul how he did it. How he lived without anger and stayed so close to Jesus with all he faced. He told me that like his biblical namesake Paul, who also suffered much, God's love empowers him every day. Listen to a man speak from beyond the grave:

> Every day we have 1,440 minutes to live. Every one of us. How much time do we spend with Him in prayer, or in sharing Him with others? I ask God every single day to come alive in my life, to make His resurrected life a reality for me. And He does it, every single day. I want a testimony of what God is doing today. People around us don't want to just hear what God is doing in your life, they want to see it! People look at my life and they are amazed? Well, my God is amazing!

Jesus was so big to Paul and eternity loomed so large that he just couldn't see much else. Evil couldn't seem to touch Paul. And now his wonderful family carries on his passion for a God-designed life and shares it with others.

The best people I have ever known understood that they were dying—that their "remaining time" was short. We know that too, don't we? Let's live like it. Like another Paul who, two thousand years ago, also had some last words for us. His last words show the balanced view of life here and life forever that we're looking for. He lived with passion to the very end and then rejoiced that it *wasn't* the end.

> For I am already being poured out like a drink offering, and the time has come for my departure. I have fought the good fight, I have finished the race, I have kept the faith. Now there is in store for me the crown of righteousness, which the Lord, the righteous Judge, will award to me on that day—and not only to me, but also to all who have longed for his appearing. (2 Timothy 4:6–8)

Imagine living that way—and dying that way. With such a sense of completion and expectation. You don't have to imagine it. Experience it! You are *meant* to.

Go ahead. Say it with Paul and believe it: "The Lord will rescue me from every evil attack and will bring me safely to his heavenly kingdom. To him be glory for ever and ever. Amen" (2 Timothy 4:18).

Safely to His heavenly kingdom. How ironic that the safest thing you can do in life is die. But that's really true for God's children. There's no safer place than His kingdom and glory—for ever and ever.

SPRINTING TO THE FINISH LINE

Real passion truly is too big for this world. God gave me a personal picture of that a few summers ago. We were vacationing on the Outer Banks of North Carolina. I was training for a half-marathon at the time, and my son and I went on a run along the beach. It was a hot but beautiful day. The waves were crashing and the sand was warm beneath our feet. We decided to try to run all the way to the Nags Head pier.

As you may know, it's often hard to tell how far away things are on the beach. The distance to that pier turned out to be a long, long way! At first, Trey and I talked and laughed as we ran. Then, as the sweat began to pour, we talked less. Pretty soon we were trudging along in silence. He began to fall behind me a little.

Finally we were only a few hundred yards from the pier. I said, "Son, I'm going to sprint the rest of the way. I'll wait for you." When I finally crossed under the pier, it felt so good to stop. I stood holding on to one of the pilings while the cool water washed over my feet.

As I looked back at my son about a hundred yards away, struggling to finish, God spoke to me. What He said moved me, and I knew it was time to share a life lesson with my son. Trey made it to the pier, and after high fives and some rest time, we sat in the sand and talked. "Trey, how did the first part of the run feel?" I asked.

"It was fun! But then it got really hot and I couldn't keep up with you."

"Yeah," I said, "but it sure felt good to finish, didn't it?"

He nodded and we sat quietly for a few minutes. "Trey, there's nothing I love more than spending time with you. And we're going to have a lot of great times together in our lives. Times when we run together side by side and it feels good. Sometimes, though, it will get harder, and I'll need to run ahead of you. I hope I'll live the kind of life you'll want to follow."

I paused. "And, son, one day—and I hope it's many years away—I'll sprint to the finish line. I might run so far ahead then that you won't see me at all. You might even think I'm gone. But don't worry about that. And don't ever be afraid of that time. I won't be gone. I'll be cheering you on as you finish your race, watching and waiting to see you cross the finish line, too."

We sat in silence for a long time, watching the ocean, just being together. Then we headed back, enjoying a relaxing walk in a beautiful place created by God—just like millions of walks I plan to take with my son when we're together in the world we were made for.

Say, why don't we plan a walk together there, too? There are many people I look forward to walking with in the next world. I bet there are a lot of things I can learn from you, and there may be a few things you can learn from me. If we're both stumped, we'll ask Jesus to join us, too. Because this is real!

A life—and an eternity—of passion waits for us. The Passion Promise is really a worldview. It's a framework for living—the core belief that directs our thoughts and actions. It's summed up well in another verse of Scripture: "For to me, to live is Christ and to die is gain" (Philippians 1:21).

We are to live our lives here on earth in all God's passion and power. He gives us a life only God can imagine. He *is* our life. And when we die, it gets even better. Now that's the life I'm after! And I bet you are, too.

chapter ten

A PROMISE KEPT

"Amen."

E ARE NEARING the end of our journey through God's Passion Promise, a promise which will change anyone who understands and believes in it. But *do* we believe? After all, promises come and go these days. It's a little scary how lightly we take our promises—even our promises to God. We go to the altar and promise God and our spouse that we will never leave each other. But if after a few years our marriage doesn't resemble a story from a romantic movie, off we go.

At New Hope, we dedicate children to the Lord three times a year. The staff explains to parents that it is also a time of parent dedication and that we will ask them to make specific promises to God. We expect them to take these commitments very seriously, and if they haven't given evidence of faithfully serving the Lord already, we hesitate to involve them in the service.

We explain to parents that we don't want to put them in a position in which they have to lie to God. What always amazes us is the number of people who don't care about this. They want the ceremony and the pictures and the little Bible even if they have no intention of keeping their promise to God.

If we break *our* important promises so easily, how do we know that God won't? Why should we trust that God has planned an amazing life of passion for us and risk that life by following Him to the edge? How do we know He won't just watch us fall?

We know because of His *Amen*. The Greek translation for *Amen* means "truly, firm, trustworthy, yes!" And that's how God ends all of His promises to us.

God has spoken His Amen many times in history, and He has always kept His promise. In that most significant promise, He said that He would send a Savior, and *He did*. He said that He would die for us, and *He did*. He said that He would conquer death, and *He did*. He said that He would forgive us, save us, and live in us and with us forever. He has and He will!

God knows you—He knows all about you. He looks at your life with love and says, "Amen! Yes. I will keep my promise to you." And God's "yes" never wavers or fails.

Think about your life for a moment. Can you see God's hand directing you at critical moments? You may have difficulty understanding many things in your life, but there are those *other* times, aren't there? Those times when you *know* that God somehow wove events together so that you are here today, so that you are who you are. He has brought you to this moment for His purpose and His passion. Your life is no accident!

FROM ALABAMA TO SIBERIA

It was 1916, and Fred Bice wanted to fight. World War I was on, and the future hung in the balance. For a wide-eyed fifteen-year-old, normal teenage life in Alabama held no appeal. He had to get to the action! To the passion! So he lied about his age, left home, made up a name for himself, and soon found himself a trained young warrior. In fact, he became a part of one of the most famous regiments in American military history—the Twenty-Seventh Infantry, the Wolfhounds. How they got that name is a part of the story.

It's a long way from Alabama to Siberia. Fred must have thought that a time or two as he trudged through the snow to engage the enemy. He was no kid now; he had become a man the hard way. He was a part of America's forgotten war—the war that continued even after World War I to protect refugees and American assets in Siberia at a time of bitter conflict between the Russian Cossacks and Bolsheviks (Communists).[11]

The Twenty-Seventh Infantry began their march through Siberia in 1918. They were fighting beside the French and the Japanese. But the French withdrew and went home, and the Japanese couldn't keep up. During one thirteen-and-a-half-hour period, the Twenty-Seventh covered fifty miles on muddy roads in a Siberian snowstorm. The major general of the Japanese army, who at the time was also commanding the Allied troops in Siberia, said that the regiment was as fierce and fleet in combat as the dog that was used to hunt wolves on the frozen wasteland—the wolfhound. (The name stuck. In 1963, U.S. Secretary of the Army Cyrus Vance declared it the official designation of the Twenty-Seventh Infantry.)

In early 1919, the Wolfhounds marched toward the city of Posolskaya, where the Cossacks were under the command of a brutal man named Gregori Semenoff. Semenoff and his men tortured, raped, and decapitated innocent Siberians.[12] They controlled the Trans-Siberian Railroad, using armored trains filled with machine-gun-equipped troops. They had to be stopped, and the Wolfhounds were called on to do it.

Young PFC Fred Bice, known by everyone as Homer Tommie, volunteered along with his best friend, Sgt. Carl Robbins, to take out the train. In total darkness, they ran toward the enemy. Then they heard gunfire. They'd been seen—they were under attack!

Bice and Robbins made it to the train. They began throwing grenades at the engine. Mission accomplished! But not without great cost. Robbins was shot and killed. Bice was hit by a grenade and fell under the train, his leg blown off. To be sure that he was dead, a Cossack stabbed him in the chest with a bayonet—missing his heart by an inch.

Some time later, the battle was won. But then came the grisly task of recovering the bodies. Bice was found, apparently dead, and placed on a cart with other bodies. But he wasn't dead. Only the slightest groan saved him from a premature burial.

The young soldier returned to the United States and recovered. He was showered with medals. His name ranks today among several Wolfhounds honored with the Distinguished Service Cross. It is still listed as Homer Tommie.

There are hundreds of accounts of courage on the battlefield just like Fred Bice's. Why is his story so special? The answer to that question takes me back to a favorite boyhood memory and the small town of Opelika, Alabama.

I can still smell the smoke from Pop's pipe as it drifts on the warm summer breeze toward the edge of the Alabama lake. "Pop, it won't bite me, will it?" I ask.

"No, Johnny, crickets don't bite. Here, I'll show you how to put it on the hook. You'll always catch bigger fish with a cricket than a worm. Now you try.... Good! You did it! Now cast that out there and hold on to that pole."

The man I knew as "Pop" was my grandfather. His real name was Fred Bice.

How close I came to never being born! Yet God, in His passionate purpose, allowed Pop to become an old man, to teach me how to fish and how to live, and to give me the finest mother I know. This is our sovereign God, the God who has said "Amen" over your life. The God who is even now weaving together the events of yesterday, today, and tomorrow to make your life count.

I could never match Pop's passion and courage. But I hope there is some Wolfhound in me. Listen to the words of Hugh O'Reilly, who wrote *Wolfhound Reflections*:

The saga of the Wolfhounds is an unending one. They have left their mark throughout the South Pacific, on the Korean Peninsula, in the jungles of Viet Nam. They were heard too in struggles of the more distant past—mountains and villages of the Philippines, and the windswept steppes of Siberia echoed with their fire and stored their actions in their memories. Wherever the nation's honor and interest were at stake the Wolfhounds were in the forefront. But not for acclaim.

Theirs has always been a higher goal. The Wolfhounds are proud warriors. They calmly bear the deep-throated roar and thunderous crash of heavy artillery, the choked cough of the mortar punctuated by the crack of rifle shots. They have always moved toward the sound of the guns, always between the enemy and their country. Over dramatic? There are no men like these! If these are your thoughts, please put these pages down. Leave us to our lives, leave us to our memories and dreams that only warriors understand.[13]

Always a higher goal. Warriors moving toward the sound of the guns. Sounds like passion to me. Sounds like the kind of life I'm after! *Thank You, God, for Your Amen! Thank You for Your promise—for this incredible gift called life. Jesus, I want to be a wolfhound for You!*

GOD AT GROUND ZERO

I thought about Pop on September 11, 2001, about how his kind of courage was going to be needed in America again. Less than a week later, through an amazing series of events that could only have been imagined by God, I was standing on the heap of the World Trade Center at Ground Zero.

A body had been recovered, and I was there to pray.

Machinery stopped, hard hats came off, and workers and volunteers fell silent as we spoke to God.

Then the recovery efforts resumed, and the man's battered body was taken away. I stood there for a long time, in the midst of the heat that melted some people's shoes, and the smoke, and the destruction that looked like hell itself.

We were briefed as we first arrived at Ground Zero. Someone told us, "Most of the bodies will never be recovered. They are dust. So walk carefully. With every step you take, you are walking through the lives of people."

It struck me at that moment that either God is real and He has a promise to keep to us even here, *even now*, or else He's not here at all and nothing in this world really matters. Which is it?

Standing there at the center of one of the worst disasters in our history, I *knew* that God was real! I felt Him even there—*especially* there. I heard Him, and you can, too. His answer for a messed-up, evil-ridden world was spoken long before September 11, and He speaks it to us every day.

His answer is everything that defines the word *Amen*. True. Firm. Trustworthy. *Yes!*

YES, I WILL MAKE THINGS RIGHT

God's Amen says that evil does not get the final word. Not even close. If you knew that in the next five minutes you were going to be faced with evil and injustice, but that for the rest of your life, you would experience only that which is right and good, wouldn't you take that offer? Of course.

The last word of the Bible is *Amen*—yes. It is God's way

of saying that in the end, right and good will triumph.

God concludes His Word with the book of Revelation. He says, in essence:

> "I am coming back to this world, and I will bring with me justice and goodness forever. The world had its five minutes of evil, and now I have all eternity to make things right! I will make right every evil ever done. I will judge. And I will reward. Amen!"

Amen! Yes! That's His answer to a world crying out for justice.

When the recent battle in Iraq began, President Bush gave a powerful speech that was clearly intended for the Iraqi people. He said, "The tyrant will soon be gone. The day of your liberation is near!"

I smiled when I heard those words. The president was absolutely right. But his statement applied to a much more dangerous threat than Saddam Hussein.

There *is* an evil tyrant in this world. He wreaks havoc on everything he touches. He is our enemy. He hates us. He hates our God. He lies, steals, and destroys. He is after you, your family, and your church. But the tyrant will soon be gone!

The day of liberation is near. Our enemy, the devil, is going down, and God will make things right.

YES, YOU CAN LIVE WITH JOY

The phrase "for ever and ever" is followed by an "Amen" twelve times in the New Testament. All twelve times the words are used in the context of absolute joy in spite of the circumstances. For instance, from prison Paul writes, "And my God will meet all your needs according to his glorious riches in Christ Jesus. To our God and Father be glory for ever and ever. Amen" (Philippians 4:19–20).

To be sure we get it, three times the Bible doubles up the word *Amen*, and all three times the context is overflowing joy and worship. Psalm 72:19 says it: "Praise be to his glorious name forever; may the whole earth be filled with his glory. *Amen and Amen.*"

"Yes and yes!" God says. You *can* live with joy in any circumstance.

My friend Gary is living proof. It was November 21, 2002, and Gary's wife, Bonnie, was opening the prenatal clinic where she served as a missionary in Sidon, Lebanon. She was preparing to serve tea and cookies to the Muslim women from a nearby Palestinian refugee camp who would be coming for treatment.

Bonnie was there to love. But a man full of hate had followed her to the clinic that morning. He shot her three times in the head. A missionary husband soon learned that his wife, only thirty-one years old, was dead.

Soon after, Gary and I met for the first time, and just a few weeks after his wife died he stood in front of my church and shared his heart. It was riveting. Television and newspaper reporters were there. What they heard was so powerful that one reporter had to be comforted by our people. It was a turning point in the life of our church. I don't think any of us there that day have ever been quite the same.

Gary stood before us, and in a voice that could barely be

heard, he said, "I stand before you as a man with nothing. I have no wife. I have no home. I have no possessions. But I have Jesus. And He is the rock beneath my feet. I stand on Him!"

As we sat amazed, Gary explained that he did not hate this man who had killed his wife, but would like to meet him and embrace him and share the love of Jesus with him. With fire in his eyes, he said, "They should have killed me too, though, because now I will never shut up about Jesus!"

I took Gary to lunch not long ago. I told him that I was concerned about him. That I hoped he was doing all right and was dealing with the natural emotions he must be feeling. He interrupted me, placed a hand on my arm, and said, "John, I know what you're worried about. You're wondering if I'm going to become angry with God over time or doubt my faith. Stop worrying! I rejected anger as an option on the day this happened. I am heartbroken, but I am passionate about the opportunity God has given me, and I will live in the joy of the Lord!"

Amen! Case closed. God is real, even in the worst thing you will ever face. And yes, you can live with joy—no matter what.

YES, MY PROMISE IS TRUE

If you need any more reason to believe His promise, here it is: "These are the words of the *Amen*, the faithful and true witness, the ruler of God's creation" (Revelation 3:14).

Jesus doesn't just say Amen. He *is* your Amen. He didn't just send His condolences to a sinful world. He came to it. He died for it. And now, no matter how bad things get, this world is not out of control but is under His control, for He is "the ruler of God's creation."

You can trust God to keep His Promise to you. And for the rest of your life, even in those times when you are walking through the world's rubble, stop and listen. For when you are tempted to wonder if He is there at all, you will hear His whisper to you, "Yes, My child, I am here. My answer to you is yes." Amen!

God has said His Amen. Now it is time for you to say yours—to say your yes to Him. The Passion Promise won't matter much to you personally until you do. Say yes to Him—now! Say yes to being a person of authentic passion. Remember what that means?

- Say, "Yes, I will focus on the Creator."
- Say, "Yes, I will reject imitations."
- Say, "Yes, I will always expect joyful passion."
- Say, "Yes, I will intentionally share genuine passion."

That's the road God has paved ahead of you. It's a good road. Not always an easy road, but never a boring road. By now, I hope you believe, with me, that it's the only road worth taking.

A while back, I was preparing to go on a writing retreat to work on this book. My plate was full; I was tired; and to be honest, I was a little discouraged about some things (not bored, mind you, just discouraged).

I regularly challenge our church members to walk or jog around our facilities at least once a week and pray. That day it was my time to prayer-run, but it was raining. I decided maybe a run in the rain would do me good. After a mile or so, I began to worship. I sought to practice what I preach and not let circumstances rob me of my joy.

As I made my second lap, the sun began to shine through the thick clouds. Suddenly I stopped in my tracks. It couldn't be! But there it was. Not one but two rainbows—a double—forming right over our church. I stood there as it grew before my eyes until its brilliant colors seemed to fill the sky.

I was so overwhelmed that I could no longer run. I couldn't even stand. I fell to my knees and lifted my hands toward the sky—toward my awesome God. The rain continued to fall and mixed with the tears running down my face. You see, for decades the rainbow has been the symbol of our church—New Hope. All of our literature, business cards, signs—everything—have rainbows on them. I had been here six years and had never seen a rainbow near our church. And now here it was, covering me, embracing our building like the arms of God.

I soon learned that church members all over town had seen it and had all thought the same thing—that God's awesome blessing and undeserved love was resting over us. But I thought about something else as well. That I had a book to finish—a book about God's *promise!*

So I got up and kept running—right under the rainbow. I ran and laughed. I ran and sang. I ran and rejoiced. For I knew that I didn't have to go somewhere over the rainbow to find a place where dreams come true. I had something better than that—a Person! One who does far more than what I can dream. He gives me a passionate life that only He can imagine.

He'll give the same to you. It's His promise.

CONCLUSION

*R*EMEMBER THAT SOUTHEAST Asian jungle village we talked about at the beginning of this book? The place where no one had even heard the name *Jesus* before? I want to take you back there now....

The mist had just begun to rise, revealing the beautiful, green mountains that surrounded us as we walked the dirt path through the village. We crossed a bridge over a small river where women went about the mundane business of washing clothes.

But there was nothing mundane about this moment. The God of the universe had a message for this village, and we were His messengers. Our hearts pounded with every step as we walked and prayed, "Oh God, open the door! You love these people more than we do. You made them for Yourself. Build Your church among these people. Begin it today!"

From the shadows of the trees two teenage girls stepped out and began talking with our interpreter, who was not much older herself. Soon we were following these teenagers to their hut, where we met their father and mother. We sat on the floor and drank a strange-tasting tea while we got to know our new friends. Our interpreter periodically glanced out the window to be sure no one had followed us.

I knew it was time. I began to explain to this family why we had traveled to their village from the other side of the world. We had come to tell them of the one true God. As the interpreter reminded them that even listening to us was dangerous, the father interrupted and said, "If you are here to tell us about God, we are not afraid of the police. We have waited so long to know about Him, but no one would tell us!"

How do you begin telling the story of the ages to people who have never heard? We started with Creation and for the next hour or two we taught. As I watched the wonder in their eyes, I felt as if I were hearing this good news for the first time, too. Our awesome Savior, the mighty King, the One who had suffered so much on our behalf—Jesus was here! He was real, and His passion filled the room.

"Have you ever heard the name Jesus?" I said.

"No. Who is he?" asked the father.

"He is the One we have been telling you about. He is God, and Jesus is His name."

"Jesus," he said.

Then each of them—father, mother, and two daughters—said "Jesus" with a smile. Our group looked in amazement at each other as we realized what had just happened. The Name above all names had been spoken by the people of this village for the first time—ever!

We told His story. How He came to earth. How He lived, died, and rose for them. How He then sent us to tell them about His love. When we finished, the father turned to our interpreter and said with astonishment, "Is this real or a fairy tale?"

"It's real!" she said. "Jesus has changed my life!"

"Then," the father said, "we have found the true God we have waited to know for so long."

A few moments later, as we knelt together on the bamboo floor, Jesus birthed His church in that village. And in heaven the joy of the angels was unleashed. In hell, the hate of the enemy raged in vain. For there would be no stopping it now. The message of the Passion Promise had come here and would not be contained.

A few weeks later, a missionary living in that country began a careful program of discipleship. For safety's sake, he took just one member of the family out of the village to be taught. It was one of the teenage girls whom we call Wa. Never in her life had she left her village. As they drove into the city, teeming with people and buildings, Wa's eyes filled with wonder.

She was taken to a home where she met several missionaries. They showed her the *JESUS* film in her language. For the first time, Wa experienced the story of her newfound

Lord. When she saw the scene of the Crucifixion, she fell on her knees. She wept and cried out, "Why are they doing that to Jesus?"

She kept watching until the Resurrection. When she saw Jesus, Wa jumped up and ran around the room, shouting to each missionary, "He's alive! He's alive! He's alive!"

He really *is* alive—and that can *mean* something in your life. More than a Sunday sermon, more than songs to sing, more than rules to keep, more than you've ever imagined. For the passion of the One who ignited the fire of the stars burns in you, calls to you, pursues you just as He pursued the Ephesians so many years ago:

> Now to him who *is* able to do immeasurably more than all we ask or imagine, according to his power that is at work within us, to him be glory in the church and in Christ Jesus throughout all generations, for ever and ever! Amen. (Ephesians 3:20–21)

These words are the foundation of the Passion Promise— that wonderful, unalterable truth that will bring joy and power to your life and your eternity: *You are designed for a life of passion—a life only God can imagine.*

That promise is yours for the journey. It's not a promise of an easy life, but of a life that counts. It's a promise for a journey that is uncertain, unsafe, and sometimes filled with pain. But it is also God's promise that He will never abandon you along the road. You will always be able to count on His presence and His passion.

Isn't that what you're really after? Can't you feel the longing of your heart for that life right now? Then look around you. God is pointing you to a life of passion at this very moment. Will you go there? Good! I hope to meet you along the way.

The publisher and author would love to hear your comments about this book. *Please contact us at:* www.multnomah.net/johnavant

Endnotes

1. Robertson, A.T. "Commentary on Ephesians 3:20." *Robertson's Word Pictures of the New Testament.* http://bible.crosswalk.com/Commentaries/RobertsonsWordPictures/rwp.cgi?book=eph&chapter=003&verse=020 (accessed 30 October 2003). Broadman Press 1932, 1933, Renewal 1960.
2. *The Complete Biblical Library, Volume 8* (Chicago: R. R. Donnelley and Sons Co., 1989): 131.
3. Ibid., 197.
4. C. S. Lewis, *The Weight of Glory* (New York: Macmillan, 1949), 3.
5. A. W. Tozer, as quoted by Literature Ministries International, "Insight for Leaders." http://www.gospelcom.net/lmi/tozer.php3?date=08-09-03 (accessed 14 October 2003).
6. David Bryant, *Toward Revival* column, "Out of Boredom—and into Rebellion," September/October 2000. Http://copi.gospelcom.net/writings/praymag/pm020.html (accessed 14 October 2003).
7. Vance Havner, *The Secret of Christian Joy* (Old Tappan, N.J.: Fleming H. Revell Co., 1938), 9.
8. Bruce Wilkinson, *The Dream Giver* (Sisters, Ore.: Multnomah, 2003), 77–8.
9. Statistic from Southern Baptist Council on Family Life, as quoted in *Rick Warren's Ministry ToolBox,* Issue 73, 10 October 2002. http://www.pastors.com/RWMT/printerfriendly.asp?issue=73&wholething=1 (accessed 16 October 2003).
10. C. S. Lewis, *Mere Christianity* (New York: Macmillan, 1952), 120.
11. U.S. National Archives & Records Administration, "Guarding the Railroad, Taming the Cossacks: The U.S. Army in Russia, 1918–1920, Part 2," by Gibson Bell Smith. http://www.archives.gov/publications/prologue/print-_friendly.html?page=winter_2002_us_army_in_russia (accessed 10 October 2003).

12. Doughboy Center, "AEF Siberia" by Christine L. Putnam. http://www.worldwar1.com/dbc/siberia/htm (accessed 13 October 2003).
13. Hugh F. O'Reilly, "Wolfhound Reflections II," 1996, 1997. http://www.kolchak.org/SGM/whnref2.htm (accessed 13 October 2003).